School Wide Book Events

School Wide Book Events

How to Make Them Happen

Virginia Lawrence Ray

A Member of the Greenwood Publishing Group
Westport, Connecticut • London

Library of Congress Cataloging-in-Publication Data

Ray, Virginia Lawrence.
School wide book events : how to make them happen / by Virginia Lawrence Ray.
p. cm.
Includes bibliographical references.
ISBN 1-59158-038-2 (alk. paper)
1. School libraries—Activity programs. 2. Children—Books and reading. 3. Reading promotion. 4. Language arts (Elementary)—Activity programs. I. Title.
Z675.S3R284 2003
027.8—dc21 2003047724

British Library Cataloguing in Publication Data is available.

Library of Congress Catalog Card Number: 2003047724
ISBN: 1-59158-038-2

First published in 2003

Libraries Unlimited, Inc., 88 Post Road West, Westport, CT 06881
A Member of the Greenwood Publishing Group, Inc.
www.lu.com

Printed in the United States of America

The paper used in this book complies with the Permanent Paper Standard issued by the National Information Standards Organization (Z39.48-1984).

10 9 8 7 6 5 4 3 2 1

Dedicated to the staff and students at

Catamount Elementary School

For sharing all those Book Events with me

Contents

Acknowledgments

For over twenty-five years I was privileged to serve as teacher and then librarian at the Catamount Elementary School in Bennington, Vermont. Every day I was fortunate to be able to work with two of my favorite things—young people and books. My thanks to the staff and students at Catamount for the hours we spent together enjoying literature. Special thanks to Norma McShane who first taught me about RIF and to Linda Bidwell and Sherry Silver for always being willing to help carry out my ideas.

I wish to thank my husband Al and my family for their steady encouragement. I am especially grateful to my daughter Kelly Ahlfeld for her insistence that I had ideas to share and for her constant faith that I could write a book.

My thanks to Ann Smith, Linda Donigan, Chris Poggi, and all my other librarian friends for sharing thoughts and letting me browse their shelves. I thank Lea Newman for her expertise as an author and a resource on Robert Frost.

I am indebted to my editor Sharon Coatney and the many supportive people at Libraries Unlimited for their guidance, patience, and good humor at various stages of this process.

Introduction

Nothing is more satisfying for a librarian than observing a child lost in the wonders of a book. Whether the child is engrossed in the magical kingdom of Narnia or caught up in the excitement of stock car racing, the mind is responding to the printed word. The imagination is stirred, pictures are formed in the brain, and learning occurs. Unfortunately, the pressures of contemporary life have forced the love of reading books further and further back on a child's agenda. After-school sports and activities absorb the child's free time. Technology has lured the child into computer games and action videos. Thus, librarians and teachers find themselves searching for ways to incorporate a love for books into the busy child's life.

Children love celebrations. They love planning for special events, participating in them, and remembering them afterward. What better way to encourage reading than to combine books and celebrations in the child's mind? And what better way to celebrate than with the whole school?

With ever-increasing curriculum demands, classroom teachers are so busy fitting all necessary subjects into the school day that they find little time to coordinate their activities with other classes. Teachers welcome the opportunity to promote language arts activities through simple schoolwide themes, but they have little time to plan them. The library offers an excellent opportunity for this coordination of literature and reading with a schoolwide theme.

School librarians have the unique ability to provide this link for the students and staff of their buildings. Because librarians deal with the school as a whole, they usually know everyone and they know the building schedule. They can plan a book event for the entire school around a specific theme and lead the celebration. The library itself is a warm, welcoming room with space for many students so grade levels can be combined to share age-appropriate materials. With a little planning, librarians can organize a book event around a simple theme that will involve everyone in the school.

It is my proposal that the librarians plan simple Book Events for their school each year. They will need to clear their schedule for the day of the event. Those working on a traditional fixed schedule will need to make other arrangements for the regular classes. Those working under flexible schedules will need to plan accordingly to do the same. It will be necessary to clear the date with school administrators and announce the event through schoolwide announcements or teacher handouts. The librarians will invite the entire school to the event on the same day, combining grade levels as library space permits. This probably will require several repetitions of the event during the day, allowing about forty minutes with each group. At the end of the day, the entire school will have been united through books and a single theme.

A book event can be planned around special days in the literary calendar such as Children's Book Week and Read Across America Day. Children can join together to celebrate a favorite author's birthday. Schools that participate in the federal "Reading Is Fundamental" (RIF) grants require program ideas to accompany the gift of books to their students several times a year. Summer Reading Programs beg to be introduced with a motivational fanfare. Special seasons in the school year or shared curriculum units provide ready-made themes for a Book Event. And sometimes no special reason is needed at all—it's just so nice to get together over books. Students will see their classmates and teachers enjoying and discussing books and want to read themselves.

In my years as a K–6 librarian, I planned "Reading Is Fundamental" programs three times a year, emphasizing reading with all students. Each program was centered on a simple theme. I found that book circulation increased after each theme activity. I came to recognize the special value of each program when faculty and students would comment to me how much fun they had at RIF. I realized how supportive teachers were in becoming involved in the presentations, providing theirs was a simple contribution. Often teachers welcomed the opportunity to challenge special students in their classes with artistic projects or creative writing opportunities. And when the classrooms became even a little bit involved in the preparations, the presentations turned into real learning situations that continued after the day of the activity.

It is my hope that this book will inspire fellow librarians and teachers to bring their whole school together in similar book celebrations and that they will feel it was truly worth the effort. The first chapter includes the basic steps involved in creating Book Events. The following chapters provide simple plans for specific themes. Bibliographies of suggested books are divided into primary and intermediate groups and included with each theme. Librarians may use these book lists for suggestions but are encouraged to add favorites of their own. Books from one grade level list may be used with other grade levels if deemed appropriate. The whole idea is to share a love of books with the whole school and have fun doing it.

1

Getting Started

Because educators agree that encouraging students to read books is a necessity and that building school unity is a worthy goal, they welcome Book Events that combine these efforts. Librarians can help to achieve these goals by planning simple schoolwide get-togethers with literature themes. Using their creativity and organizational skills (areas in which librarians excel), they can plan a Book Event for their entire student body. The event should be held in the school library, surrounded by books. Students may be divided into manageable groups to fit the space available, and the program can be repeated throughout the same day with age-appropriate variations. Classes enjoy contributing to the celebrations in small ways such as artistic, written, or dramatic pieces. The whole school will be discussing the same theme, children will be reading more books, and everyone will have a good time.

The following is a brief summary for planning a Book Event:

Basic Steps for Creating Book Events

1. Choose a broad theme. Many are suggested in the chapters that follow. Themes should appeal to all age groups within the school. Select one that sounds like fun to you—your enthusiasm will be infectious.

2. Discuss the event with school administrators and ask them to help select an appropriate date—an entire morning, if possible. Be sure that the date doesn't conflict with events such as field trips or concerts. Request that students be allowed to attend the Book Event if it falls during their special classes of art, gym, or music. Perhaps the special teacher will be allowed to bring them to the event if the classroom teacher is busy. Clear the library of all other commitments for that morning, being careful to notify teachers well ahead of time of any changes. Reschedule commitments if necessary. It is important that teachers feel good about the coming Book Event so that they communicate the anticipation to their students.

3. Set up the schedule, grouping several grade levels as library space permits. Allow forty-five minutes for each group and at least fifteen minutes between groups. Possible groups could include grades K–2, 3–4, and 5–6. (The number of groups necessary depends upon the size of the library and the number of students.)

4. Two weeks before the event, invite administrators, teachers, and students through a written handout, including the schedule. Printing the invitation on brightly colored paper or decorating it will make it special. On the invitation, request a simple, theme-related contribution (a drawing, a poem, a question, a photo, etc.) from each class—not necessarily each student. One or two from a class is fine. Suggested contributions accompany

the themes in this book. This contribution helps each class become more involved in the celebration, increases anticipation, and provides a focal point for the event itself. Ask them to send contributions to the library a week before the Book Event.

5. Search the library for theme-related books. Bibliographies accompany each theme in this book. Choose books on all grade levels. Often picture books are useful for all ages. Display books near a bulletin board area.

6. Design a motivational bulletin board display around the theme, incorporating student contributions. This should be near the area where the event will be held. The bulletin board provides a visual focal point for discussion and helps each class feel a part of the event. Having the bulletin board up a few days early increases anticipation for the day; leaving it up for a couple of weeks after the event will extend the learning of the day and encourage students to read more books on the theme.

7. Plan the event, remembering always to read books to the students and involve them in discussing the theme. The actual program will depend upon the theme. Some themes may lend themselves to social studies or science activities, while others invite participation in music or art. Sometimes an outside speaker is appropriate. Sometimes it's fun to involve the students in a little skit. Program ideas are included in the following chapters.

8. Order simple theme-related bookmarks or small tokens to give the students as they leave the activity. It is important to extend the learning of the day if possible, and a bookmark can remind the students afterward. Bookmarks are relatively inexpensive and stress the importance of reading. Library catalogs offer such a wide selection of bookmarks that usually one can be found to match the theme.

9. Remind teachers of the schedule ahead of time. Life gets very busy in the classroom, and everyone needs a little reminder. This can be done through the school's daily announcements for several days before the Book Event. The schedule for the event may be rather tight, and it's better to remind folks ahead of time than have them late for the program.

10. Have a wonderful time!

2

Solve a Mystery: Who Stole the Cookies from the Cookie Jar?

THEME: Mystery Books

PURPOSE: To encourage students to explore mystery books

MATERIALS:

Selection of mystery books at all reading levels

Cookie jar (a large, sturdy, clear jar, with cover)

Cookies

STUDENT CONTRIBUTION:

Solution to the mystery of who stole the cookies

Preparation for Book Event

TWO WEEKS BEFORE THE BOOK EVENT, send out an invitation to students and staff.

Everyone is invited to a Book Event celebrating mystery stories at the library. You will be challenged to follow the clues and solve a mystery yourself. The folks at the library have even baked a big batch of cookies as a reward. Come and play detective with us.

Make the bulletin board display. Place a huge question mark in the middle of the board. Surround it with jackets from mystery books. Attach words such as WHO? WHERE? HOW? WHY? WHEN? Add a trail of large footprints and a magnifying glass cut from construction paper.

Set up a book display of mystery titles to encourage students to read. The bibliographies at the end of this chapter offer suggestions.

During library classes or school announcements, arouse students' interest by showing them a full cookie jar. Explain that the cookies will be shared for the Book Event.

Arrange with a fun-loving staff member to be the "guilty party" who will "steal" the cookies. (They do not have to actually steal the cookies—they will be guilty in name only and will redeem themselves.)

A WEEK BEFORE THE BOOK EVENT, announce to everyone that the cookies have disappeared. The jar has been found empty. Issue the challenge to solve the mystery of who stole the cookies. You will provide clues daily as you discover them. Encourage students to come to the library to discover clues on their own, write their mystery solutions on slips of paper, and put them in the empty cookie jar.

Clues may include:

The cover was removed and placed on the right side of the jar.
(Culprit is right-handed.)

Crumbs were found on the bookcase next to the empty jar.
(The culprit ate the cookies near the jar.)

A blond hair was discovered on the floor.
(Culprit is blond.)

Crumbs were found in a certain spot in the hall outside the library.
(Culprit's room is in that direction.)

A small slip of paper with a single letter of the alphabet on it was found on the floor.
(Initial of the culprit.)

A book that did not belong to the library was discovered on the shelf beside the empty jar.
(Title should point to interests of the culprit.)

Book Event Activity

Wear a trench coat with collar up, Sherlock Holmes type hat, and carry a magnifying glass. Use the bulletin board to explain that the theme for the day is mystery books. Discuss what happened to the cookies. Pull several student solutions at random from the jar.

Play the rhythmic chanting game "Who Stole the Cookies from the Cookie Jar?"

Librarian: (Choosing teacher's name in the group)
Mrs. Brown stole the cookies from the cookie jar!

Mrs. Brown: Who, me?

Librarian: Yes, you!

Mrs. Brown: Not me! Couldn't be!

Librarian: Then who?

Mrs. Brown: (Choosing name from the group)
Bobbie stole the cookies from the cookie jar!

Bobbie: Who, me? (Repeat rest of jingle)

Everyone joins in to play the game, adding new names as they chant.

Suddenly the "guilty" staff member rushes in with plastic bags of cookies, saying, "Oh, I hope I'm on time! I have your cookies! I took them home and put them in the freezer because I was afraid they would get stale before you had a chance to eat them. You probably didn't even notice they were gone!"

The cookies are placed on the shelf to be shared at the end of the activity. The librarian uses a cookie story to lead into a discussion of mystery stories in general, using books that have been selected and displayed in full view. (See bibliography at end of this chapter.)

The librarian reads a short mystery book and/or a few students may act out a role-play they have prepared for the group. After the books and the role-plays, students select books and enjoy a cookie.

SUGGESTED MYSTERY ROLE-PLAY 1 (GRADES K–3)

The Nail Polish

Stephanie: Mom, I can't find my new red nail polish.

Mom: Where did you leave it?

Stephanie: In the bathroom—but it's gone!

Mom: Did you look in the bedroom?

Stephanie: Yes, but it's not there.

Mom: Did you look in your backpack?

Stephanie: Yes, but it's not there.

Mom: I'll help you look after lunch. Will you please call your brothers for lunch now?

Stephanie: O.K. Johnny! Bobby! It's lunchtime!

(Johnny and Bobby enter. Johnny carries a red model car; Bobby carries a book.)

Mom: Sit down for lunch, children. Put your toys down on the shelf.

Bobby: O.K., Mom. (Puts book down.)

Johnny: Mom, I can't. My car needs to dry before I can set it down. (Waves it in air and blows on it.)

Mom: I think I have solved the mystery, Stephanie. I know what happened to your nail polish.

QUESTION TO AUDIENCE: Where is the nail polish? How did Mom know?

ANSWER: Johnny used it to paint his car. The paint was still wet.

SUGGESTED ROLE-PLAY 2 (GRADES 4–6)

The Skateboard

Sherlock (Sitting in office, reading detective magazine.)

Paula: (Bursting into the office). Sherlock, I need your help!

Sherlock: What's the problem?

Paula: Someone has stolen my skateboard!

Sherlock: (Grabbing magnifying glass). Well, let's see if we can solve this mystery. Where did you last see your skateboard?

Paula: I left it under the apple tree.

Sherlock: Well, let's go look around for clues. Oh, here comes your brother. Maybe he can help us.

(Joe enters)

Joe: Hi. What are you two doing?

Paula: Looking for my skateboard. It's missing!

Joe: Well, don't look at me. I haven't been near the apple tree all day.

Sherlock: That's not quite true. You were there at least once when you took Paula's skateboard.

QUESTION TO AUDIENCE: How did Sherlock know that Joe was guilty?

ANSWER: Joe said he hadn't been near the apple tree all day. Paula had never told him she lost it near the apple tree.

Suggested Bibliography for Mystery Theme

Primary Grades

Adler, David A. *Young Cam Jansen and the Baseball Mystery.* New York: Viking Press, 1999.

Berenstain, Stan. *The Bear Detectives: The Case of the Missing Pumpkin.* New York: Beginner Books, 1975.

Byars, Betsy Turner. *Herculeah Jones* mystery series. London: Puffin, 1997.

Clement, Rod. *Grandpa's Teeth.* New York: HarperCollins, 1997.

Hearne, Betsy Gould. *Who's In the Hall?: A Mystery in Four Chapters.* New York: Greenwillow Books, 2000.

Hurd, Thacher. *Art Dog.* New York: HarperCollins, 1996.

Jonas, Ann. *The 13th Clue.* New York: Greenwillow Books, 1992.

Kellogg, Steven. *The Mystery of the Stolen Blue Paint.* New York: Dial Press, 1982.

Kitamura, Satoshi. *Sheep in Wolves' Clothing.* New York: Farrar, Straus and Giroux, 1996.

Naylor, Phyllis Reynolds. *Ducks Disappearing.* New York: Atheneum Books for Young Readers, 1997.

Nixon, Joan Lowery. *Gus and Gertie and the Missing Pearl.* New York: SeaStar Books, 2000.

Park, Barbara. *Junie B. Jones and Some Sneaky Peeky Spying.* New York: Random House, 1994.

Rylant, Cynthia. *The High-Rise Private Eyes: The Case of the Puzzling Possum.* New York: Greenwillow Books, 2001.

Schertle, Alice and Margot Tomes. *Witch Hazel.* New York: HarperCollins, 1991.

Sharmat, Marjorie Weinman. *Nate the Great and the Big Sniff.* New York: Delacorte Press, 2001.

Skofield, James. *Detective Dinosaur.* New York: HarperCollins, 1996.

Stevenson, James. *The Mud Flat Mystery.* New York: Greenwillow Books, 1997.

Van Allsburg, Chris. *The Stranger.* Boston: Houghton Mifflin, 1986.

Wick, Walter. *I Spy Mystery: A Book of Picture Riddles.* New York: Scholastic Books, 1993.

Intermediate Grades

Adler, David A. *Cam Jansen and the Barking Treasure Mystery.* New York: Viking, 1999.

Creech, Sharon. *Chasing Redbird.* New York: HarperCollins, 1997.

Dixon, Franklin W. *The Secret Panel.* New York: Grosset & Dunlap, 1974. (And other Hardy Boys books in the series.)

Fleischman, Sid. *Jim Ugly.* New York: Greenwillow Books, 1992.

Hahn, Mary Downing. *The Dead Man in Indian Creek.* New York: Clarion Books, 1990.

Howe, Deborah and Alan Daniel. *Bunnicula: A Rabbit Tale of Mystery.* New York: Atheneum, 1979.

Keene, Carolyn. *The Haunted Bridge.* Bedford, MA: Applewood Books, 2000. (And other Nancy Drew books in the series.)

Kehret, Peg. *Nightmare Mountain.* New York: Dutton, 1989.

Lisle, Janet Taylor. *Looking for Juliette.* New York: Orchard Books, 1994.

Logan, Claudia. *The 5,000-Year-Old Puzzle: Solving a Mystery of Ancient Egypt.* New York: Farrar, Straus and Giroux, 2002.

Newman, Robert. *The Case of the Baker Street Irregular: A Sherlock Holmes Story.* New York: Atheneum, 1978.

Roberts, Willo Davis. *The Kidnappers: A Mystery.* New York: Atheneum Books for Young Readers, 1998.

Simon, Seymour. *Einstein Anderson, Science Detective* series. New York: Morrow, 1997.

Sobol, Donald J. *Encyclopedia Brown Finds the Clues.* New York: Bantam Skylark Books, 1994.

Van Allsburg, Chris. *The Mysteries of Harris Burdick.* Boston: Houghton Mifflin, 1984.

Voigt, Cynthia. *The Vandemark Mummy.* New York: Atheneum, 1991.

Warner, Gertrude Chandler. *Tree House Mystery.* Chicago: A. Whitman, 1969. (And other Boxcar Children mysteries in series.)

Yolen, Jane. *The Mary Celeste: An Unsolved Mystery from History.* New York: Simon & Schuster Books for Young Readers, 1999.

3

Places to Go

THEME: Books about travel

PURPOSE: To excite students about exploring their world through books

MATERIALS:

Large world map

Posters of different countries

Selection of fiction and nonfiction books about different countries

Bookmarks illustrating places in the world

STUDENT CONTRIBUTIONS:

Construction paper hot air balloon

Riddles about countries of the world

Wearing T-shirts from vacation spots

Preparation for Book Event

TWO WEEKS BEFORE THE BOOK EVENT, inform staff and students that there will be a Book Event on world travel.

Come to a World Travel Book Event in the library. Everyone is invited to wear a T-shirt from some vacation spot. Please have your class draw one hot air balloon onto brightly colored paper and compose at least one riddle about a place in the world. Riddles should be short and descriptive. For example:

Grades K–3: I am a country of the world. Kangaroos live in my country. What am I?
Grades 4–6: I am a country in Europe. I am shaped like a boot. I am near the Mediterranean Sea. What am I?

Please write the answers to the riddles on the reverse side of the questions. The balloons and riddles should be brought to the library by the end of this week. Come and discover the world.

Order bookmarks illustrating places in the world.

A WEEK BEFORE THE BOOK EVENT, design a bulletin board with a large world map in the middle and the hot air balloons all around it. Put pictures of other countries on or near the bulletin board. Add large construction paper letters for the caption, THE PLACES YOU'LL GO!

Place the students' riddles in a small briefcase or duffel bag near the bulletin board. Make up extra riddles yourself to add to the collection.

Arrange a display of fiction and nonfiction books about other countries.

Book Event Activity

On the day of the Event wear a T-shirt from some vacation spot. Welcome students and staff by reading *Oh, the Places You'll Go!* by Dr. Seuss.

Discuss the bulletin board and places to which the audience may have traveled. Have some souvenirs available to show from your own or another staff member's travels. Select someone to use a pointer or place a marker on the world map as specific countries are mentioned.

Draw several riddles from the bag. Have students guess the answers.

Explain to the students that the riddles will be available for them to solve on their own for the next few weeks in the library.

Discuss the displayed fiction and nonfiction books on countries of the world.

Read a short fiction book with a foreign setting or an excerpt from a nonfiction book.

As they leave, give each student a bookmark picturing a place in the world.

Suggested Bibliography for Travel Theme

Primary Grades

Bemelmans, Ludwig. *Madeline's Rescue.* New York: Viking Press, 1953.

Binch, Caroline. *Gregory Cool.* New York: Dial, 1994.

Bogart, Jo Ellen and Barbara Reid. *Gifts.* New York: Scholastic Books, 1994.

Brown, Don. *Alice Ramsey's Grand Adventure.* Boston: Houghton Mifflin, 1997.

Brown, Norman. *Clifford Takes a Trip.* New York: Scholastic Books, 1966.

Crews, Donald. *Sail Away.* New York: Greenwillow Books, 1995.

Gackenbach, Dick. *With Love from Gran.* New York: Clarion Books, 1989.

Hobbie, Holly. *Toot and Puddle.* Boston: Little, Brown, 1997.

Lewin, Ted. *Amazon Boy.* New York: Macmillan, 1993.

Mason, Margo and Dale Gottlieb. *Are We There Yet?* New York: Bantam Books, 1990.

McMillan, Bruce. *One Sun: A Book of Terse Verse.* New York: Holiday House, 1990.

Neitzel, Shirley and Nancy Winslow Parker. *The Bag I'm Taking to Grandma's.* New York: Mulberry, 1998.

Prelutsky, Jack and Yossi Abolafia. *What I Did Last Summer.* New York: Greenwillow Books, 1984.

Priceman, Marjorie. *How To Make an Apple Pie and See the World.* New York: Knopf, 1994.

Rey, Margret. *Whiteblack the Penguin Sees the World.* Boston: Houghton Mifflin, 2000.

Seuss, Dr. *Horton Hatches the Egg.* New York: Random House, 1940.

———. *I Had Trouble Getting to Solla Sollew.* New York: Random House, 1993.

———. *Oh, the Places You'll Go!* New York: Random House, 1990.

Smith, Maggie. *Counting Our Way to Maine.* New York: Orchard Books, 1995.

Stanley, Diane and Elise Primavera. *Moe the Dog in Tropical Paradise.* New York: Putnam, 1992.

Tews, Susan. *Lizard Sees the World.* New York: Clarion Books, 1997.

Intermediate Grades

Anno, Mitsumasa. *Anno's Italy.* New York: Collins, 1978.

Blumberg, Rhoda. *Shipwrecked: True Adventures of a Japanese Boy.* New York: HarperCollins, 2001.

Cities of the World series. Chicago: Children's Press, 1997. (Or similar series.)

Countries: Faces and Places series. Chanhassen, MN: Child's World, 1998. (Or similar series.)

Countries of the World series. Milwaukee, WI: Gareth Stevens, 1998. (Or similar series.)

Creech, Sharon. *Walk Two Moons.* New York: HarperCollins, 1994.

———. *The Wanderer.* New York: HarperCollins, 2000.

Danziger, Paula. *You Can't Eat Your Chicken Pox, Amber Brown.* New York: Putnam, 1995.

Dewey, Jennifer. *Antarctic Journal: Four Months at the Bottom of the World.* New York: HarperCollins, 2001.

Fascinating Facts: Cultures Around the World. Lincolnwood, IL: Publications International, 1992.

Fleming, Candace. *Gabriella's Song.* New York: Atheneum, 1997.

Fox, Paula. *Lily and the Lost Boy.* New York: Orchard Books, 1987.

Garland, Sherry. *Lotus Seed.* Orlando, FL: Harcourt Brace, 1993.

Geraghty, Paul. *The Hunter.* New York: Crown, 1994.

Handford, Martin. *Where's Waldo Now?* Cambridge, MA: Candlewick Press, 1997.

Heinz, Brian J. and Gregory Manchess. *Nanuk: Lord of the Ice.* New York: Dial, 1998.

Isadora, Rachel. *Over the Green Hills.* New York: Greenwillow Books, 1992.

Leedy, Loreen. *Postcards from Pluto: A Tour of the Solar System.* New York: Holiday House, 1993.

Moss, Marissa. *Amelia Hits the Road.* Middleton, WI: Pleasant Company, 1999.

Parker, Lewis K. *Japan.* Vero Beach, FL: Rourke Book Co., 1994.

Raskin, Lawrence. *52 Days by Camel: My Sahara Adventure.* Toronto: Annick Press, 1998.

Shepard, Aaron and Daniel San Souci. *The Gifts of Wali Dad: A Tale of India and Pakistan.* New York: Atheneum, 1995.

Sis, Peter. *Tibet: Through the Red Box.* New York: Farrar, Straus and Giroux, 1998.

Williams, Vera B. and Jennifer Williams. *Stringbean's Trip to the Shining Sea.* New York: Greenwillow Books, 1988.

4

Pet Lovers

THEME: Fiction and Nonfiction Books about Pets and Pet Care

PURPOSE: To encourage students to use library books to learn about animals and how to care for them

MATERIALS:

Selection of fiction and nonfiction books about many types of pets

Large pictures of pets

Pet bookmarks or animal stickers

STUDENT CONTRIBUTIONS:

Snapshot or drawing of their pet

A can of pet food, a pet toy, or an old towel

Preparation for Book Event

THREE WEEKS BEFORE THE BOOK EVENT, contact the local humane society or animal shelter and request a volunteer speaker for the day of the activity. Ask for someone who is experienced in addressing children about proper care of pets. Suggest that fifteen to twenty minutes would be appropriate. Explain the Book Event schedule so the speaker will understand that it will be necessary to repeat the message at different grade levels.

TWO WEEKS BEFORE THE BOOK EVENT, begin announcements to the students and staff.

> The theme for our next Book Event is "Pet Lovers." Staff and students are invited to bring snapshots or drawings of their own pets to the library within the next week. All snapshots and drawings should be labeled with the name of the student, classroom teacher, and pet. Come and celebrate pets with us.

As the pictures arrive, attach them to a bulletin board without damaging them. (A room divider bulletin board makes the pictures easy for everyone to study.) Double-faced tape will do the job. Another method is to place them in plastic photo album sheets that can then be tacked to the bulletin board. Label the bulletin board with a sign such as "We Care for Our Pets."

Create a collage of pictures of all sorts of pets on a large bulletin board. Old calendars often have wonderful pictures of cats and dogs especially. Try to find pictures of reptile, amphibian, fish, and bird pets along with the more familiar mammals. Label the bulletin board "Pets Are Special."

Purchase pet bookmarks or animal stickers.

A WEEK BEFORE THE BOOK EVENT, confirm the speaker from the humane society. Send the speaker specific directions and a time schedule. Inform the students about the speaker and suggest that they bring a donation of a can of pet food, a pet toy, or an old towel (for animal bedding) to the event. These donations will be presented to the speaker for the animals in the shelter and will give the students an opportunity to help care for homeless pets. Locate a carton or two to hold the donations.

Collect fiction and nonfiction titles about pets, and arrange a display. Be sure to include books on pet care and nature guides. Search words might include cat, dog, horse, ferret, fish, mouse, iguana, guinea pig, hamster, gerbil, lizard, parakeet, turtle, hermit crab, and rabbit.

Book Event Activity

Wear a T-shirt or outfit with animals pictured on it. Let the office know you are expecting a speaker from the humane society. Place the empty cartons near the door of the library for the donations.

Greet the students and staff. Read a short picture book about pets to the group. Suggestions:

Grades K–2: *The Last Puppy* by Frank Asch or *The Aminal* by Lorna Balian.

Grades 3–6: *Martha Speaks* by Susan Meddaugh or *Stories To Read To Your Dog (Cat)* by Sara Swan Miller.

Thank them for the snapshots, drawings, and the donations to the animal shelter. Call their attention to the bulletin boards and the book display. Introduce the speaker from the humane society, who will speak about "Caring for Pets" for about fifteen to twenty minutes. Allow a few minutes afterward for questions and answers. Thank the speaker and present the gifts for the shelter. Read students a short poem about pets. Shel Silverstein and Jack Prelutsky, among others, have written humorous poems on the subject. Present students with pet bookmarks or animal stickers as they leave.

SUGGESTED BIBLIOGRAPHY FOR PET THEME

PRIMARY GRADES

Abercrombie, Barbara. *Charlie Anderson.* New York: Aladdin Paperbacks, 1995.

Asch, Frank. *The Last Puppy.* Englewood Cliffs, NJ: Prentice-Hall, 1980.

Balian, Lorna. *The Aminal.* Watertown, WI: Humbug Books, 1994.

Bemelmans, Ludwig. *Madeline's Rescue.* New York: Viking Press, 1975.

Blake, Robert J. *Akiak: A Tale from the Iditarod.* New York: Philomel Books, 1997.

Bridwell, Norman. *Clifford, the Big Red Dog.* New York: Scholastic Books, 1988.

Brunhoff, Laurent de. *Babar and the Wully-Wully.* New York: H. Abrams, 2001.

Calhoun, Mary. *Blue-Ribbon Henry.* New York: Morrow Junior Books, 1999.

Capucilli, Alyssa. *Biscuit.* New York: HarperTrophy, 1997.

Carbonnet, Gabrielle. *Boodil, My Dog.* New York: Henry Holt, 1995.

Casely, Judith. *Mr. Green Peas.* New York: Greenwillow Books, 1995.

Gag, Wanda. *Millions of Cats.* New York: Penguin Putnam Books for Young Readers, 1996.

Howe, James. *Pinky and Rex and the Just-Right Pet.* New York: Atheneum Books for Young Readers, 2001.

McMillan, Bruce. *Mouse Views: What the Class Pet Saw.* New York: Holiday House, 1993.

Meddaugh, Susan. *Martha Speaks.* Boston: Houghton Mifflin, 1992.

Miller, Sara Swan. *Three Stories You Can Read to Your Dog.* Boston: Houghton Mifflin, 1995.

Park, Barbara. *Junie B. Jones Smells Something Fishy.* New York: Random House, 1998.

Rylant, Cynthia. *Henry and Mudge and Annie's Perfect Pet: The Twentieth Book of Their Adventures.* New York: Simon & Schuster Books for Young Readers, 2000.

———. *Mr. Putter & Tabby Toot the Horn.* San Diego: Harcourt Brace, 1998.

———. *The Old Woman Who Named Things.* San Diego: Harcourt Brace, 1996.

Sierra, Judy. *There's a Zoo in Room 22.* San Diego: Harcourt, 2000.

Zolotow, Charlotte. *The Old Dog.* New York: HarperCollins, 1995.

Intermediate Grades

Abercrombie, Barbara. *Charlie Anderson.* New York: Aladdin Paperbacks, 1995.

Adler, David A. *Cam Jansen and the Catnapping Mystery.* New York: Viking, 1998.

Ames, Lee J. *Draw 50 Animals.* New York: Doubleday, 1974.

Blake, Robert J. *Akiak: A Tale from the Iditarod.* New York: Philomel Books, 1997.

Caryn, Jenner. *Black Beauty.* New York: DK Publishers, 1997.

Coville, Bruce. *Jeremy Thatcher, Dragon Hatcher.* San Diego: Jane Yolen Books, 1991.

DiCamillo, Kate. *Because of Winn-Dixie.* Cambridge, MA: Candlewick Press, 2001.

George, Jean Craighead. *How To Talk to Your Cat.* New York: HarperCollins, 2000.

———. *On the Far Side of the Mountain.* New York: Dutton Children's Books, 1990.

Haas, Jessie. *Beware the Mare.* New York: Beech Tree, 1996.

Howe, Deborah. *Bunnicula: A Rabbit-Tale of Mystery.* New York: Atheneum Books for Young Readers, 1999.

Jenner, Caryn. *Black Beauty.* New York: Alfred A. Knopf, distributed by Random House, 1993.

Levy, Elizabeth. *Night of the Living Gerbil.* New York: HarperCollins, 2001.

Lowry, Lois. *Anastasia, Absolutely.* New York: Bantam Doubleday Dell Books for Young Readers, 1997.

Meddaugh, Susan. *Martha Speaks.* Boston: Houghton Mifflin, 1992.

Miller, Sara Swan. *Three Stories You Can Read to Your Cat.* Boston: Houghton Mifflin, 1997.

———. *Three Stories You Can Read to Your Dog.* Boston: Houghton Mifflin, 1995.

Naylor, Phyllis Reynolds. *Shiloh.* New York: Aladdin Paperbacks, 2000.

Rawlings, Marjorie Kinnan. *The Yearling.* New York: Aladdin Classics, 2001.

Selden, George and Garth Williams. *Harry Cat's Pet Puppy.* New York: Farrar, Straus and Giroux, 1974.

Warner, Gertrude Chandler. *The Pet Shop Mystery.* Morton Grove, IL: A. Whitman, 1996.

5

Hats Off and On

THEME: Books about Hats

PURPOSE: To challenge students to design their own hats through tales involving hats

MATERIALS:

Hat representing a fictional character for librarian to wear on the activity day (e.g., Amelia Bedelia, Cat in the Hat, Old King Cole)

Variety of hats for display

Selection of books and stories featuring hats

Bookmarks featuring hats or reading

STUDENT CONTRIBUTIONS:

Wear a hat representing a fictional character for the activity day.

Colored paper cutouts of all kinds of hats. Each class can contribute two or three cutouts.

Preparation for Book Event

TWO WEEKS BEFORE THE BOOK EVENT, explain to the staff that there will be a Book Event featuring hats.

> It's a Hat Day Book Event at the library! Please have several students in your class make large colored paper cutouts of any type of hat. They should bring these cutouts to the library by the end of this week. Everyone is invited to wear a hat to the Book Event to represent a character in a book or story. These hats can be created for the occasion or simply taken from the closet at home. Because the fun will be in guessing the character's identity, please try to keep it a secret. There will be books and stories available in the library to help students select a character if they need suggestions.

Design a bulletin board to look like a hat shop. Cut out construction paper hat stands (slender pedestals with small circles at top.) Make large letters to spell HAT SHOPPE. Attach several paper hats at random on the board. Add hats as students send them to the library. Place a few hats on display near the bulletin board.

Ask several students and/or staff members to help you dramatize the story *Caps for Sale* by Esphyr Slobodkina during the Book Event. If possible these actors should be available to do the play for each group at the Book Event. Otherwise you can choose different actors for each group presentation. You will need:

- A Reader (the librarian, the principal, or a teacher)
- The Peddler (an older student or a teacher)
- Five Monkeys (small students)

As the reader narrates the story, the peddler and the monkeys act it out. Do not be too concerned with elaborate costumes or setting. Acting out the story should be fun and require little preparation. You will need to rehearse it with the monkeys once before the Event. A large chair can represent the tree under which the peddler falls asleep. The monkeys can sit in little chairs behind the peddler. The peddler must wear several hats, one on top of another during parts of the presentation. The monkeys pretend they are in trees, except for the time they snitch the caps.

Set up a collection of books and stories about hats to stir students' and teachers' imaginations.

Order bookmarks featuring hats or the joy of reading.

A WEEK BEFORE THE BOOK EVENT, remind everyone to select their hats. Encourage staff privately to wear hats on the day of the activity.

Rehearse the peddler skit.

THE DAY BEFORE THE BOOK EVENT, issue a final reminder to wear hats the next day.

Book Event Activity

Wear a hat representing a fictional character. Even dress like the character if the spirit moves you! Welcome everyone by showing a red hood or scarf. Ask the students to name a story character who wore such an item. Discuss the familiar tale of *Little Red Riding Hood* briefly. Then read *Little Red Cowboy Hat* by Susan Lowell. Thank those who have worn hats. Ignore the fact that there are those who didn't. Participation will increase as students become more comfortable with Book Events.

Discuss the hats on the bulletin board and the hats on display. Point out several of the books in which characters wear specific hats. Invite those who have worn hats to stand one at a time while others guess which fictional character they represent. Be lavish with compliments. It will increase participation the next time around.

Dramatize the story *Caps for Sale* by Slobodkina. Read the story aloud while volunteers act it out.

Give each student a bookmark as they leave.

Suggested Bibliography for Hat Theme

Primary Grades

Agee, Jon. *Milo's Hat Trick.* New York: Hyperion Books for Children, 2001.

Asch, Frank. *Happy Birthday, Moon.* Englewood Cliffs, NJ: Prentice-Hall, 1982.

Barrett, Judi. *Animals Should Definitely Not Wear Clothing.* New York: Atheneum, 1970.

Bemelmans, Ludwig. *Madeline and the Bad Hat.* New York: Viking Press, 1956.

Blackaby, Susan. *Rembrandt's Hat.* Boston: Houghton Mifflin, 2002.

Brett, Jan. *The Hat.* New York: Putnam, 1997.

Diakite, Baba Wague. *The Hatseller and the Monkeys: A West African Folktale.* New York: Scholastic Books, 1999.

Fox, Mem. *The Magic Hat.* San Diego, CA: Harcourt, 2002.

Gardella, Tricia. *Casey's New Hat.* Boston: Houghton Mifflin, 1997.

Hanel, Wolfram. *The Extraordinary Adventures of an Ordinary Hat.* New York: North-South Books, 1995.

Lear, Edward and Jill Newton. *Of Pelicans and Pussycats: Poems and Limericks.* New York: Dial Books for Young Readers, 1990.

Levy, Janice. *The Man Who Lived in a Hat.* Charlottesville, VA: Hampton Roads Publishers, 2000.

Lowell, Susan. *Little Red Cowboy Hat.* New York: Henry Holt, 1997.

Nodset, Joan L. *Who Took the Farmer's Hat?* New York: HarperCollins, 1988.

Polacco, Patricia. *Chicken Sunday.* New York: Philomel Books, 1992.

Rey, H.A. *Curious George.* Boston: Houghton Mifflin, 1993.

Seuss, Dr. *The Cat in the Hat.* New York: Random House, 1957.

———. *The 500 Hats of Bartholomew Cubbins.* New York: Random House, 1990.

Slobodkina, Esphyr. *Caps for Sale: A Tale of a Peddler, Some Monkeys & Their Monkey Business.* New York: W.R. Scott, 1947.

Stoeke, Janet Morgan. *A Hat for Minerva Louise.* New York: Dutton Children's Books, 1994.

Tafuri, Nancy. *Silly Little Goose!* New York: Scholastic Books, 2001.

Intermediate Grades

Carlson, Laurie M. *Boss of the Plains: The Hat That Won the West.* New York: DK Ink, 2000.

Fleming, Candace and Robert Andrew Parker. *The Hatmaker's Sign: A Story by Benjamin Franklin.* New York: Orchard Books, 1998.

Glass, Andrew. *Bewildered for Three Days: As To Why Daniel Boone Never Wore His Coonskin Cap.* New York: Holiday House, 2000.

Jockel, Nils. *Pieter Bruegel's Tower of Babel: The Builder with the Red Hat.* New York: Prestel, 1998.

Kalman, Bobbie. *Bandannas, Chaps, and Ten-Gallon Hats.* New York: Crabtree, 1999.

Kimmel, Eric A. *I-Know-Not-What, I-Know-Not-Where: A Russian Tale.* New York: Holiday House, 1994.

Krisher, Trudy and Nadine Bernard Westcott. *Kathy's Hats: A Story of Hope.* Morton Grove, IL: A. Whitman, 1992.

Meddaugh, Susan. *Lulu's Hat.* Boston: Houghton Mifflin, 2002.

Newman, Jerry. *Green Earrings and a Felt Hat.* New York: Henry Holt, 1993.

Peters, Stephanie True. *Hat Trick.* Boston: Little, Brown, 2000.

Tripp, Valerie. *Kit's Home Run.* Middleton, WI: Pleasant Company, 2002.

Walker, Niki. *The Milliner.* New York: Crabtree, 2002.

6

Tall Tales

THEME: Tall Tales of Folklore

PURPOSE: To interest students in reading and writing tall tales

MATERIALS:

Selection of tall tales from library shelves

Large posters of tall tale characters such as Paul Bunyan and Pecos Bill (often available through library supply catalogs)

Four large-mouth plastic containers (i.e., pitchers or large water bottles) of different colors

Paper in colors matching the containers cut into strips $8\frac{1}{2}" \times \frac{3}{4}"$

One sheet of poster board

Laminating film and laminator

Theme-related bookmarks

STUDENT CONTRIBUTION:

Strips of paper on which they have written CHARACTERS, THINGS, PLACES, or DEEDS.

Preparation for Book Event

TWO WEEKS BEFORE THE BOOK EVENT, notify staff and students that there will be a celebration of tall tales in the library.

Bring your imaginations to the library for the next Book Event. We are going to create some quick Tall Tales. Please have your class return to the library the attached strips of colored paper, on which they have written imaginary CHARACTERS, THINGS, PLACES, or DEEDS. Note the specific category for your grade level and the following examples. Be sure to use the colored paper attached to this notice. Please send the slips to the library sometime this week.

Grades K and 1: Write the name of an imaginary CHARACTER such as a doctor, Mrs. Rushmore, a racecar driver, or a baker.
Grades 2 and 3: Write the name of a THING such as a baseball bat, a bouquet of yellow flowers, a birthday cake, or a purple dragon. Use describing words.
Grade 4: Write the name of a PLACE such as a desert, California, the Pacific Ocean, or a shopping mall. Be descriptive.
Grades 5 and 6: Write an amazing DEED that someone might have accomplished such as built a skyscraper, played in the Super Bowl, traveled to Mars, or slept for a year. Be imaginative. Please write in the past tense.

It is important to assign a specific color for each of the four categories so that the slips may be organized in matching containers for student use. Give each class approximately ten strips of colored paper upon which to write their contributions.

Order theme-related bookmarks.

A WEEK BEFORE THE BOOK EVENT, construct a bulletin board display entitled TALL TALES. Place a large figure of Paul Bunyan in the center surrounded by other folklore characters. Label each character with his or her name.

Label the four plastic containers with CHARACTERS, THINGS, PLACES, and DEEDS. Laminate the slips of paper from the classes and place them in the corresponding containers.

Use the poster board to make a story template by writing the following in large print:

Once upon a time ____________ took ____________ to
(character) *(thing)*

____________ and ____________.
(place) *(deed)*

Search the library stacks for tall tales and arrange a display. Choose specific tales to read aloud at the event.

Book Event Activity

Dress like a tall tale character or wear a T-shirt emphasizing reading. Welcome everyone to a celebration of exaggeration. Begin by telling a tall tale of your own such as:

You'll never believe what my day has been like. When I woke up, it was completely dark outside. The sun had forgotten to come up! So I had to go outside in my pajamas and bedroom slippers and holler at that sun to wake up and get going. It took fifty-seven big yells before that sun finally came over the mountain. By then it was getting kind of late, so I had to hurry my breakfast. I only had time for three bowls of cereal, seven slices of toast, and a half-gallon of tomato juice to wash it all down. I figured I'd probably be hungry before lunch ever got here, so I tucked a dozen doughnuts into my pocket just in case. I hitched my pet gorilla to the clothesline and told him to hang out the laundry. Then I jumped on my jet-propelled motor scooter and zipped off to school. Whew! What a day it's been already!

Ask the students to comment on the story, leading into a discussion of tall tales. Discuss the bulletin board and library book displays. Explain that tall tales told the history of our country and the hard-working people trying to tame it. Some tall tale characters such as Davy Crockett and Johnny Appleseed were real persons, but others like Paul Bunyan and Pecos Bill were fictionalized characters of tales told by loggers and cowboys. Each story became bigger and more exaggerated each time it was told until finally it was written down.

Read a picture book such as *Paul Bunyan* or *Pecos Bill* by Steven Kellogg. Discuss briefly how these stories may have originated.

Explain that the students can create their own tall tales. Display the plastic containers containing the slips of paper the students contributed. Read the story template aloud, asking students to draw a slip from the proper container for each blank as you come to it. Students may read the slips themselves or hand them to you to be read. Encourage the students to imagine what would happen next in the tale. Do several repetitions of the template, each time pulling new slips from the containers. Explain that the slips will remain in the library for the next few weeks for students to use on their own. If they would like to write them down, the tales will be posted in the library to share with others.

Close the program by reading another tall tale such as *Johnny Appleseed by* Steven Kellogg, *John Henry* by Julius Lester, *The Bunyans* by Audrey Wood, or *Harvey Potter's Balloon Farm* by Jerdine Harold Nolen and Mark Buehner.

Give students theme-related bookmarks as they leave.

Suggested Bibliography for Tall Tales Theme

Primary Grades

Adler, David. A. *A Picture Book of Davy Crockett.* New York: Holiday House, 1996.

Barrett, Judi. *Cloudy with a Chance of Meatballs.* New York: Atheneum, 1978.

Fleischman, Sid. *A Carnival of Animals.* New York: Greenwillow Books, 2000.

Harper, Jo. *Outrageous, Bodacious Boliver Boggs!* New York: Simon & Schuster Books for Young Readers, 1996.

Isaacs, Anne and Paul O. Zelinsky. *Swamp Angel.* New York: Dutton Children's Books, 1994.

Kellogg, Steven. *Johnny Appleseed: A Tall Tale.* New York: Morrow Junior Books, 1988.

———. *Paul Bunyan.* New York: William Morrow, 1984.

———. *Pecos Bill.* New York: Morrow Junior Books, 1986.

Ketteman, Helen. *Luck with Potatoes.* New York: Orchard Books, 1995.

Nolen, Jerdine Harold and Mark Buehner. *Harvey Potter's Balloon Farm.* New York: Lothrop, Lee & Shepard Books, 1994.

Roth, Susan L. *The Biggest Frog in Australia.* New York: Simon & Schuster Books for Young Readers, 1996.

Schanzer, Rosalyn. *Davy Crockett Saves the World.* New York: HarperCollins, 2001.

Shepard, Aaron. *Master Man: A Tall Tale of Nigeria.* New York: HarperCollins, 2001.

Stefanec-Ogren, Cathy. *The Adventures of Archie Featherspoon.* New York: Aladdin, 2002.

Thomassie, Tynia and Cat Bowman Smith. *Feliciana Feydra LeRoux: A Cajun Tall Tale.* Boston: Little, Brown, 1995.

Wood, Audrey and David Shannon. *The Bunyans.* New York: Blue Sky Press/Scholastic Books, 1996.

Intermediate Grades

Benet, Rosemary. *Johnny Appleseed.* New York: M.K. McElderry, 2001.

Blair, Walter. *Tall Tale America: A Legendary History of Our Humorous Heroes.* New York: Coward-McCann, 1944.

Feeney, Kathy. *Davy Crockett: A Photo-Illustrated Biography.* Mankato, MN: Bridgestone Books, 2002.

Fleischman, Sid and Eric Von Schmidt. *Jim Bridger's Alarm Clock and Other Tall Tales.* New York: E.P. Dutton, 1978.

Fleischman, Sid and Kurt Werth. *McBroom and the Big Wind.* New York: Norton, 1967.

Kellogg, Steven. *Johnny Appleseed: A Tall Tale.* New York: Morrow Junior Books, 1988.

———. *Mike Fink: A Tall Tale.* New York: Morrow Junior Books, 1992.

———. *Paul Bunyan.* New York: William Morrow, 1984.

———. *Pecos Bill.* New York: Morrow Junior Books, 1986.

Nolen, Jerdine. *Big Jabe.* New York: Lothrop, Lee & Shepard Books, 2000.

Lester, Julius. *John Henry.* New York: Dial Books, 1994.

Osborne, Mary Pope and Michael McCurdy. *American Tall Tales.* New York: Knopf, 1991.

San Souci, Robert D. and Brian Pinkney. *Cut from the Same Cloth: American Women of Myth, Legend, and Tall Tale.* New York: Philomel Books, 1993.

Selgin, Peter. *"S.S." Gigantic Across the Atlantic: The Story of the World's Biggest Ocean Liner Ever! And Its Disastrous Maiden Voyage.* New York: Simon & Schuster Books for Young Readers, 1999.

Sis, Peter. *A Small Tall Tale from the Far Far North.* New York: Knopf, 1993.

Wood, Audrey and David Shannon. *The Bunyans.* New York: Blue Sky, 1996.

7

Bright Ideas of the Past: Inventors and Inventions

THEME: Biographies, Reference Books, and Other Nonfiction Sources

PURPOSE: To encourage students to use the library to research inventions in American history and to develop an appreciation of creative thinking

MATERIALS:

Selection of biographies and reference books relating to specific inventions and inventors in American history

Selection of picture books and fiction titles emphasizing creative thinking

Web site information on inventions, using the computer

$6^{1}/_{2}$" × $2^{1}/_{2}$" strips of tag board for bookmarks (one per student)

Laminating film and laminator

Modern telephone

STUDENT CONTRIBUTION:

Handmade bookmark on which the student has written information about an inventor and/or invention.

Preparation for Book Event

THREE WEEKS BEFORE THE BOOK EVENT, set up a display of fiction and nonfiction books about inventors and inventions in American history. Inform the staff and students that you will be honoring inventors on that day. Provide teachers with the following information and enough $6^{1/2}$" × $2^{1/2}$" blank strips of heavy paper so that each student can make a bookmark .

The library will be celebrating American Inventors and inventions at a special Book Event. A selection of books on this topic will be available in the library for student use. Please discuss inventions in your class. Students should design a bookmark about an invention on the enclosed strips of paper. On one side, list the invention, the name of the inventor, and the date of the invention. Draw a small picture to illustrate it. On the back of the bookmark, write the student's name and the teacher's name. Use pencils, crayons, and markers to make it colorful. Bring the bookmark to the library within the next two weeks. Primary grade teachers may opt to do this as a group project about a single inventor. Older students may use reference materials to research and complete the project independently. Let's see how many inventors we can discover.

A WEEK BEFORE THE BOOK EVENT, put up a bulletin board display entitled BRIGHT IDEAS. Draw a large, yellow light bulb for the centerpiece with yellow rays radiating from it. Scatter names of inventions about the bulletin board. Illustrate the inventions with pictures, if possible. Along the edges of the board, put the names of the inventors. Number each inventor and invention with the same number so that students may enjoy matching them.

Laminate the students' bookmarks and sort them by classroom.

Ask two students to assist in the Alexander Graham Bell skit. Have them each make a telephone prop: a tag board cylindrical megaphone set atop a circular cardboard base, with a few wires attached. Drawings of this early telephone are available in reference books. Practice the skit once to make the students comfortable.

Select books to be used for the Book Event.

Book Event Activity

Wear a T-shirt symbolic of an invention or an expression of creativity. Welcome the group by holding up a light bulb and asking whose bright idea it was (Thomas Edison's). Discuss the bright ideas on the bulletin board and have students match the inventors with their inventions.

Perform the following skit about the invention of the telephone with the assistance of two students.

SKIT ABOUT ALEXANDER GRAHAM BELL

Setting: Use a divider to separate the room into two areas, each containing a small desk holding a telephone.

Narrator: (Holding up a modern telephone.) This is a telephone. We use it all the time and don't think anything about it. We call our friends to chat. We call our doctor for an appointment. We call out for pizza. We can't remember a time when there were no telephones, but there was such a time. Before there were telephones, people wrote letters to their friends to chat. They rode in a horse and buggy to the doctor's house. And they pulled molasses taffy at home for a treat. This is the story of the invention of the telephone.

It was the year 1876. A young man named Alexander Graham Bell lived in Boston, Massachusetts. He had a job teaching deaf children to speak during the day and he worked on his science experiments at night. He was trying to invent a machine that could carry the human voice from one person to another.

(Bell enters stage and busies himself with apparatus.)

Alexander Graham Bell had an assistant who worked with him on his experiments. His name was Thomas Watson.

(Watson enters stage and moves wires around.)

One day Bell was working in his laboratory speaking into one piece of the equipment—the transmitter. Watson was in the bedroom listening to the other piece—the receiver. At first Watson could hear nothing. Then Bell spilled some acid onto his pants and shouted into the transmitter.

Bell: Mr. Watson, come here! I want to see you!

Narrator: Watson could hear him! He was so excited that he ran into the laboratory.

Watson: I could hear you, Mr. Bell! I could hear you!

Bell: What did I say?

Watson: You said, "Come here. I want to see you."

Bell: That's right! Let's change places and try it again.

Narrator: So Bell went into the bedroom and listened as Watson read from a book. Bell couldn't understand the words from the book but he did hear Watson when he spoke louder.

Watson: Mr. Bell, do you understand what I say?

Narrator: Then they took turns talking to each other.

Bell: How do you do?

Watson: How do you do?

Narrator: Bell even sang some music. Both men were very excited. Their experiments had finally worked and they had invented the telephone.

(Student actors take a bow and sit with audience.)

Display the packets of laminated bookmarks. Ask if there are students who remember the information on the bookmark they created. Pull a few from the packet and read the information aloud.

Ask the students to name some personal characteristics of inventors (imagination, persistence, creativity, patience, etc.) Ask them if they have ever invented anything. Encourage them to invent something and bring it to the library for a future display.

Read a simple picture book such as *Margaret Knight: Girl Inventor* by Marlene Targ Brill or *The Glorious Flight: Across the Channel with Louis Bleriot* by Alice and Martin Provensen.

Hand out the laminated bookmarks to classroom teachers as everyone leaves.

Suggested Bibliography for Inventions Theme

Primary Grades

Abraham, Philip. *Benjamin Franklin.* New York: Children's Press, 2002.

Brill, Marlene Targ. *Margaret Knight: Girl Inventor.* Brookfield, CT: Millbrook Press, 2001.

Carle, Eric. *Walter the Baker.* New York: Simon & Schuster Books for Young Readers, 1995.

Gaines, Ann. *Alexander Graham Bell.* Vero Beach, FL: Rourke, 2002.

———. *Eli Whitney.* Vero Beach, FL: Rourke, 2002.

———. *Henry Ford.* Vero Beach, FL: Rourke, 2002.

Harper, Charise Mericle. *Imaginative Inventions: The Who, What, Where, When, and Why of Roller Skates, Potato Chips, Marbles, and Pie and More!* Boston: Little, Brown, 2001.

Lewis, J. Patrick. *Isabella Abnormella and the Very, Very Finicky Queen of Trouble.* New York: DK Ink, 2000.

Priceman, Marjorie. *It's Me, Marva!: A Story About Color & Optical Illusions.* New York: Alfred A. Knopf, Distributed by Random House, 2001.

Provensen, Alice and Martin. *The Glorious Flight: Across the Channel with Louis Bleriot.* New York: Viking Press, 1983.

Reiss, Mike. *The Great Show-and-Tell Disaster.* New York: Price Stern Sloan, 2001.

Sayre, April Pulley. *Noodle Man: The Pasta Superhero.* New York: Orchard Books, 2002.

Stefanec-Ogren, Cathy. *The Adventures of Archie Featherspoon.* New York: Aladdin, 2002.

Taylor, Barbara. *I Wonder Why Zippers Have Teeth and Other Questions About Inventions.* New York: Kingfisher, 1995.

Intermediate Grades

Bowen, Andy Russell. *A Head Full of Notions: A Story about Robert Fulton.* Minneapolis, MN: Carolrhoda Books, 1997.

Bridgman, Roger Francis. *1,000 Inventions & Discoveries.* Washington, DC: DK, in association with the Smithsonian Institution, London, 2002.

Clements, Andrew. *Frindle.* New York: Simon & Schuster Books for Young Readers, 1996.

Erlbach, Arlene. *The Kids' Invention Book.* Minneapolis: Lerner, 1999.

Freedman, Russell. *The Wright Brothers: How They Invented the Airplane.* New York: Holiday House, 1991.

Fritz, Jean. *What's the Big Idea, Ben Franklin?* New York: PaperStar, 1996.

Giblin, James. *The Amazing Life of Benjamin Franklin.* New York: Scholastic Books, 2000.

Gutman, Dan. *The Edison Mystery.* New York: Simon & Schuster Books for Young Readers, 2001.

MacLeod, Elizabeth. *Alexander Graham Bell: An Inventive Life.* Toronto: Kids Can Press, 1999.

Matthews, Tom. *Always Inventing: A Photobiography of Alexander Graham Bell.* Washington, DC: National Geographic Society, 1999.

Platt, Richard. *Smithsonian Visual Timeline of Inventions.* New York: Dorling Kindersley, 1994.

Rubin, Susan Goldman. *Toilets, Toasters & Telephones.* San Diego: Browndeer Press/Harcourt Brace, 1998.

Scieszka, Jon. *Hey, Kid, Want To Buy a Bridge?* New York: Viking, 2002.

St. George, Judith. *So You Want To Be an Inventor?* New York: Philomel Books, 2002.

Thimmesh, Catherine. *Girls Think of Everything: Stories of Ingenious Inventions by Women.* Boston: Houghton Mifflin, 2000.

Wulffson, Don L. *The Kid Who Invented the Trampoline: More Surprising Stories about Inventions.* New York: Dutton Children's Books, 2001.

———. *Toys!: Amazing Stories Behind Some Great Inventions.* New York: Henry Holt, 2000.

8

Reading Solves Puzzles

THEME: Puzzle and Riddle Books

PURPOSE: To challenge students' problem-solving skills

MATERIALS:

Selection of books containing puzzles and riddles, ditto master books containing puzzles

STUDENT CONTRIBUTION:

Ideas for palindromes or hink-pinks

Preparation for Book Event

TWO WEEKS BEFORE THE BOOK EVENT, invite the staff and students.

You and your class are invited to a Mind Boggling Book Event in the library. Please discuss palindromes and hink-pinks with your class. A palindrome is a word or group of words that are spelled exactly the same backward as forward, such as MOM or MADAM I'M ADAM. A hink-pink is a word puzzle such as sad footwear = blue shoe or chubby kitty = fat cat. Hink-pink answers are synonyms that rhyme and have the same number of syllables. Have your students make up one or two examples from your class. Suggestions are available in the library if you need them. Please send your puzzles to the library by the end of this week.

A WEEK BEFORE THE BOOK EVENT, copy the puzzle suggestions onto colorful pieces of tag board for the bulletin board. Palindromes may be copied as written. Hink-pink definitions and answers should be written on separate sheets so students may work out the puzzles themselves. Add large cutout letters to spell READING SOLVES PUZZLES.

Copy approximately twenty riddles appropriate for grades K–3 and twenty riddles for grades 4–6 onto slips of paper. Write the answers in small print on the backs of the papers. Fold the slips in half and put them into separate containers for the Figure-It-Out game on the day of the event. Label the containers with the grade levels.

Photocopy a variety of puzzles from ditto master books—more than enough for all students.

Arouse interest in the event by putting a riddle or puzzle on the daily announcements for a week before the Book Event. Give correct answers on the following day.

Arrange a display of riddle and puzzle books.

Book Event Activity

Wear a reading theme T-shirt. Add some incorrect accessories for students to puzzle about, such as mismatched shoes or socks, sunglasses, one glove, or an umbrella. Welcome staff and students and ask them to figure out what is wrong with the way you are dressed. Give them an age-appropriate riddle to solve.

Discuss the bulletin board and solve the word puzzles with the group. Explain the variations in the puzzle and riddle books displayed. Read a few riddles from the books.

Challenge the group to a Figure-It-Out contest between two teams. Choose a scorekeeper to write the points on a chalkboard or poster. Explain that you have riddles written on the slips of paper in the containers. Have students select the riddles and then read the riddles to each team alternately. Record points for correct answers. Keep the stress level down and the fun level up. Stop the game before students tire and tell them that the riddles will be available for them to use independently in the library after Book Event.

Read a book to the group such as *Toll-Bridge Troll* by Patricia Rae Wolff, *Mouse Views: What the Class Pet Saw* by Bruce McMillan, or *Curious George Goes to the Hospital* by Margret Rey.

Send the students on their way with an age-appropriate puzzle that you have photocopied. Students may return to the library during the following week to check their answers.

Suggested Bibliography for Puzzle Theme

Primary Grades

Baker, Keith. *Hide and Snake.* San Diego: Harcourt Brace, 1991.

Geisert, Arthur. *Pigs from A to Z.* Boston: Houghton Mifflin, 1986.

———. *Pigs from 1 to 10.* Boston: Houghton Mifflin, 1992.

Gwynne, Fred. *A Chocolate Moose for Dinner.* New York: Aladdin Paperbacks, 1976.

———. *The King Who Rained.* New York: Aladdin Paperbacks, 1980.

Karim, Roberta. *Kindle Me a Riddle: A Pioneer Story.* New York: Greenwillow Books, 1999.

Lewis, J. Patrick. *Riddle-icious!* New York: Alfred A. Knopf, 1996.

Lyn, Thomas. *Ha! Ha! Ha! : 10001 Jokes, Riddles, Facts, and More.* New York: Firefly Books, 2001.

MacDonald, Suse. *Look Whooo's Counting.* New York: Scholastic Books, 2000

McMillan, Bruce. *Mouse Views: What the Class Pet Saw.* New York: Holiday House, 1993.

Miller, Margaret. *Guess Who?* New York: Greenwillow Books, 1994.

Moncure, Jane Belk. *Word Bird Makes Words with Cat.* Chanhassen, MN: Child's World, 2002.

Ready—Set—Read—and Laugh!: A Funny Treasury for Beginning Readers. New York: Delacorte, 1995.

Rey, Margret. *Curious George Goes to the Hospital.* Boston: Houghton Mifflin, 1994.

Stoeke, Janet Morgan. *Minerva Louise at School.* New York: Puffin, 1999.

Wolff, Patricia Rae. *The Toll-Bridge Troll.* San Diego: Harcourt Brace, 1995.

Weitzman, Jacqueline. *You Can't Take a Balloon into the National Gallery of Art.* New York: Dial Books for Young Readers, 2000.

Wick, Walter. *I Spy: A Book of Picture Riddles.* New York: Scholastic Books, 2000.

Intermediate Grades

Adler, David. *Easy Math Puzzles.* New York: Holiday House, 1997.

Agee, Jon. *Go Hang a Salami! I'm a Lasagna Hog!: And Other Palindromes.* New York: Farrar, Straus and Giroux, 1994.

Giblin, James Cross. *The Riddle of the Rosetta Stone: Key to Ancient Egypt.* New York: Thomas Y. Crowell, 1990.*

Handford, Martin. *Where's Waldo Now?* Cambridge, MA: Candlewick Press, 1997.

I Saw Esau: The Schoolchild's Pocket Book. Cambridge, MA: Candlewick Press, 1992.

Simon, Seymour. *The Gigantic Ants and Other Cases.* New York: Morrow Junior Books, 1997.

Steiner, Joan. *Look-alikes.* Boston: Little, Brown, 1998.

Swann, Brian. *The House with No Door: African Riddle-Poems.* San Diego: Harcourt Brace, 1998.

. *Touching the Distance: Native American Riddle-Poems.* San Diego: Browndeer Press, 1998.

Take Me to Your Liter: Science and Math Jokes. New York: Pippin Press, 1991.

Terban, Marvin. *Funny You Should Ask: How To Make Up Jokes and Riddles with Wordplay.* Boston: Houghton Mifflin, 1992.

———. *Too Hot To Hoot: Funny Palindrome Riddles.* Boston: Houghton Mifflin, 1976.

Van Laan, Nancy. *With a Whoop and a Holler: A Bushel of Lore from Way Down South.* New York: Atheneum, 1998.

Warner, Gertrude Chandler. *The Mystery at the Ballpark.* New York: Holiday House, 1993.

The World Almanac for Kids 2003. New York: World Almanac Education Group, 2002.

*This nonfiction book follows scholars as they solve the riddle of the Rosetta stone, which provided a key to translating the hieroglyphics of ancient Egypt.

9

Once Upon a Time...

THEME: Fairy Tales

PURPOSE: To develop appreciation of our literary heritage of fairy tales and introduce lesser-known tales

MATERIALS:

Wide selection of fairy tales from library shelves. Include modern parodies of these tales.

Bright colored pencils

STUDENT CONTRIBUTION:

A large colored cutout illustrating a symbol for a given fairy tale from each class

Preparation for Book Event

TWO WEEKS BEFORE THE BOOK EVENT, gather fairy tales and fairy tale parodies from the library shelves. Select an age-appropriate tale for each class.

Invite staff and students and request the cutout symbol for the bulletin board.

Purchase bright colored pencils, one for each student.

You are all invited to a ONCE UPON A TIME...Book Event at the library. Please read or review the following tale with your class:

____

A copy of the tale is available in the library if you need it. Discuss an appropriate symbol to represent this story to others. For example, a large slipper could represent the story of Cinderella. Have someone in your class draw this symbol on a sheet of colored paper that is twelve inches by eighteen inches and cut it out. Decorate it any way you please. Just don't add any words other than your class name on the back of the symbol. Bring it to the library by the end of this week. Let's celebrate the wonderful world of fantasy together.

A WEEK BEFORE THE BOOK EVENT, arrange the paper cutouts on a bulletin board with large letters spelling out the words ONCE UPON A TIME. Post a list of the titles illustrated in a small corner of the bulletin board as a key for those who need it.

Choose books to read to the group during the Book Event.

Book Activity Event

Wear a colorful robe and carry a magic wand to represent a wizard. Welcome everyone with a few magic words to set the tone.

Discuss characteristics of fairy tales—magic, royalty, poor people, good triumphing over evil, love, and happily-ever-after endings. Read a traditional fairy tale to the group. Ask the students to locate some of the above elements in the story.

Thank classes for making the symbols of the fairy tales for the bulletin board. Have everyone try to guess the name of the tale that goes with each symbol. Younger classes will probably not know some of the tales but can be introduced to them.

Discuss the fact that sometimes the same fairy tale varies depending upon the culture of the country where it is told. Review briefly the tale of Cinderella. Show several samples of the Cinderella story as told in different cultures. Some examples include *The Gift of the Crocodile* by Judy Sierra, *The Egyptian Cinderella* by Shirley Climo, *Princess Furball* by Charlotte S. Huck, and *Cendrillon: A Caribbean Cinderella* by Robert D. San Souci. In grades K–3, read one of the variations to the group.

In grades 4–6, discuss the origins of tales, introducing them to the Grimm brothers and Hans Christian Andersen. Explain the meaning of a parody—a humorous imitation of the original tale. Show several modern versions of traditional fairy tales, such as *The Stinky Cheese Man and Other Fairly Stupid Tales* and *The Frog Prince Continued* by Jon Scieszka, *Jack and the Beanstalk* by Richard Walker, *Little Red Cowboy Hat* by Susan Lowell, or *The Principal's New Clothes* by Stephanie Calmenson. Read one of these fractured fairy tales to the group. Encourage students to write their own parodies and submit them to the library.

Close the event with a wave of the wand and some final magic words. Give students colored pencils as magic wands of their own.

Suggested Bibliography for Fairy Tale Theme

Primary Grades

Ada, Alma Flor. *Dear Peter Rabbit.* New York: Atheneum Books for Young Readers, 1994.

Andersen, Hans Christian. *Hans Christian Andersen's Fairy Tales.* New York: North-South Books, 2001.

Aylesworth, Jim. *The Gingerbread Man.* New York: Scholastic Books, 1998.

Climo, Shirley. *The Egyptian Cinderella.* New York: HarperCollins, 1989.

———. *The Korean Cinderella.* New York: HarperCollins, 1993.

———. *The Persian Cinderella.* New York: HarperCollins, 1999.

De Paola, Tomie. *Adelita: A Mexican Cinderella Story.* New York: Putnam, 2002.

Hickox, Rebecca. *The Golden Sandal: A Middle Eastern Cinderella Story.* New York: Holiday House, 1998.

Huck, Charlotte S. *Princess Furball.* New York: Mulberry, 1994.

Kellogg, Steven. *Jack and the Beanstalk.* New York: Morrow Junior Books, 1991.

Osborne, Mary Pope. *The Brave Little Seamstress.* New York: Atheneum Books for Young Readers, 2002.

Perrault, Charles. *Cinderella, or The Little Glass Slipper.* New York: Atheneum Books for Young Readers, 1954.

Pinkney, Jerry. *The Ugly Duckling.* New York: Morrow Junior Books, 1999.

San Souci, Robert D. *Cendrillon: A Caribbean Cinderella.* New York: Simon & Schuster Books for Young Readers, 1998.

———. *The Talking Eggs—A Folktale from the American South.* New York: Dial Books for Young Readers, 1989.

Sierra, Judy. *The Gift of the Crocodile: A Cinderella Story.* New York: Simon & Schuster Books for Young Readers, 2000.

Zelinsky, Paul O. *Rapunzel.* New York: Dutton Children's Books, 1997.

Intermediate Grades

Andersen, Hans Christian. *Hans Christian Andersen's Fairy Tales.* New York: North-South Books, 2001.

Burch, Joann Johansen. *A Fairy-Tale Life: A Story about Hans Christian Andersen.* Minneapolis, MN: Carolrhoda Books, 1994.

Calmenson, Stephanie. *The Principal's New Clothes.* New York: Scholastic Books, 1989.

The Complete Grimm's Fairy Tales. New York: Pantheon Books, 1980.

Demi. *The Emperor's New Clothes: A Tale Set in China.* New York: McElderry Books, 2000.

Hogrogian, Nonny. *The Devil with the Three Golden Hairs.* New York: Alfred A. Knopf, 1983.

Johnson, Tony. *Bigfoot Cinderrrrrella.* New York: Putnam, 1998.

Kimmel, Eric A. *Iron John—Adapted from the Brothers Grimm.* New York: Holiday House, 1994.

Levine, Gail Carson. *Cinderellis and the Glass Hill.* New York: HarperCollins, 2000.

———. *Ella Enchanted.* New York: HarperCollins, 1997.

Lowell, Susan. *Little Red Cowboy Hat.* New York: Henry Holt, 2000.

McCaughrean, Geraldine. *One Thousand and One Arabian Nights.* Oxford, England: Oxford University Press, 1982.

Scieszka, Jon. *The Frog Prince, Continued.* New York: Viking, 1991.

———. *The Stinky Cheese Man and Other Fairly Stupid Tales.* New York: Viking, 1992.

Steig, Jeanne. *A Handful of Beans: Six Fairy Tales.* New York: HarperCollins, 1998.

Tharlet, Eve. *The Emperor's New Clothes.* New York: North-South Books, 2000.

A Wolf at the Door: And Other Retold Fairy Tales. New York: Simon & Schuster Books for Young Readers, 2000.

Yep, Laurence. *The Dragon Prince: A Chinese Beauty & the Beast Tale.* New York: HarperCollins, 1997.

10

Pretty Things That Are Well Said: Poems to Remember

THEME: Poetry Books

PURPOSE: To develop appreciation of poetry and challenge students to memorize a poem

MATERIALS:

Selection of poetry books and biographies of poets

Four to six posters displaying poems written in large print

Laminating film

STUDENT CONTRIBUTION:

Voluntary memorization of a short poem or verse

Preparation for Book Event

THREE WEEKS BEFORE THE BOOK EVENT, gather poetry books and biographies of poets from the shelves for a display.

Begin to motivate the school by sending an announcement to staff members.

Everyone is invited to celebrate poetry in a Book Event at the library. We will be reading a variety of poems and listening to each other recite favorite lines by heart. Years ago it was quite common to have poetry recitations in schools. Students developed self-confidence in public speaking and an appreciation for poetry. You and your class are invited to participate on a voluntary basis. The entire class can speak as a group or several students in the class can recite individually. Primary grades may want to consider nursery rhymes. Books of poetry are available in the library for suggestions. All students should have their poems approved by their teacher or the librarian. During the next two weeks, please let me know the names of those willing to participate and the titles of their poems.

Pretty things that are well said—
It's nice to have them in your head.

ROBERT FROST*

*Frost, *Look Magazine* (March 31, 1959) from an untitled quatrain never collected in his published works

TWO WEEKS BEFORE THE BOOK EVENT, choose poem posters for the bulletin board. Library and school supply companies often have such posters for sale or you may choose to make your own in large print on colorful backgrounds. Select a variety of poems covering primary and intermediate grade level interests. Cut out large block letters that spell PRETTY THINGS THAT ARE WELL SAID for the bulletin board.

Encourage staff and students to memorize a poem by speaking to them individually and by using daily announcements.

Choose a poem to memorize yourself. It may be just a couple of verses, but it sets an example for the students and staff.

Select one or two poems for each grade level. Copy them onto colored paper, laminate them, and cut them into card-size mementos, one for each student.

A WEEK BEFORE THE BOOK EVENT, check with teachers to be sure you have an accurate list of participants and poem titles. Develop the order of poem recitations for the Event. Select other poems you will read during the Event.

Put up the bulletin board display.

Book Event Activity

Dress up for the occasion to create the feeling that poetry is a special writing style.

Welcome everyone by reading several short poems from the sources listed in the bibliographies. Choose a variety of poems from light and humorous to descriptive and moving. You may want to read the poems you have laminated as mementos. Include a Robert Frost poem such as "The Pasture." Then repeat the excerpt from the Robert Frost quatrain previously quoted in the invitation to the Book Event.

> Pretty things that are well said—
> It's nice to have them in your head

Discuss the meaning of the lines. Ask the students if it was difficult to memorize the lines they have prepared. Set up an atmosphere of acceptance in the room by discussing what it means to be a good audience. Everyone should be quiet, maintain eye contact with the person speaking, and applaud when the person is finished. Recite the poem you have memorized as an example. Following the program you have set up earlier, invite those who have memorized verses to stand in front of the group and share their poems. Thank each participant after the poem is recited. When everyone is finished, praise the group for adding "pretty things that are well said" to their memory banks. Encourage everyone to do this independently.

Read the poems posted on the bulletin board and discuss the poetry books available in the display, including the biographies of poets. If time allows, read another poem from the collections. A picture book version of a longer poem such as Robert Frost's "Stopping by Woods on a Snowy Evening" would be a nice way to end the program.

As the students leave, give each one a laminated poem card to remember the occasion.

Suggested Bibliography for Poetry Theme

Primary Grades

Animal Crackers: A Delectable Collection of Pictures, Poems, Songs, and Lullabies for the Very Young. Boston: Little, Brown, 1996.

Bedard, Michael. *Emily.* New York: Doubleday Books for Young Readers, 1992.

Big, Bad and Little Bit Scary: Poems That Bite Back! New York: Viking, 2001.

Fleming, Denise. *The Everything Book.* New York: Henry Holt, 2000.

Florian, Douglas. *Beast Feast.* San Diego: Harcourt Brace, 1994.

———. *Summersaults: Poems & Paintings.* New York: Greenwillow Books, 2002.

Good Books, Good Times! New York: HarperCollins, 1990.

Graham, Joan Bransfield. *Splish Splash.* New York: Ticknor & Fields Books for Young Readers, 1994.

Hoberman, Mary Ann. *You Read to Me, I'll Read to You: Very Short Stories To Read Together.* Boston: Little, Brown, 2001.

Michael Foreman's Mother Goose. San Diego: Harcourt Brace, 1991.

Prelutsky, Jack. *Awful Ogre's Awful Day: Poems.* New York: Greenwillow Books, 2001.

———. *Beneath a Blue Umbrella.* New York: Greenwillow Books, 1990.

———. *The Frogs Wore Red Suspenders.* New York: Greenwillow Books, 2002.

The Random House Book of Poetry for Children. New York: Random House, 1983.

Sylvia Long's Mother Goose. San Francisco: Chronicle Books, 1999.

Updike, John. *A Child's Calendar: Poems.* New York: Holiday House, 1999.

Zemach, Margot. *Some from the Moon, Some from the Sun: Poems and Songs for Everyone.* New York: Farrar, Straus and Giroux, 2001.

Intermediate Grades

Classic Poems To Read Aloud. New York: Kingfisher, 1995.

Cooper, Floyd. *Coming Home: From the Life of Langston Hughes.* New York: Philomel Books, 1994.

Dickinson, Emily. *A Brighter Garden: Poetry.* New York: Philomel Books, 1990.

Frost, Robert. *Stopping by Woods on a Snowy Evening.* New York: Dutton Children's Books, 2001.

———. *A Swinger of Birches: Poems of Robert Frost for Young People.* Owings Mills, MD: Stemmer House, 1982.

Hesse, Karen. *Out of the Dust.* New York: Scholastic Books, 1997.

Janeczko, Paul B. *How To Write Poetry.* New York: Scholastic Reference, 1999.

King, Sarah E. *Maya Angelou: Greeting the Morning.* Brookfield, CT: Millbrook Press, 1994.

The Oxford Illustrated Book of American Children's Poems. New York: Oxford University Press, 1999.

Poetry by Heart: A Child's Book of Poems To Remember. New York: Scholastic Books, 2001.

Prelutsky, Jack. *Ride a Purple Pelican.* New York: Greenwillow Books, 1986.

Silverstein, Shel. *A Light in the Attic.* New York: HarperCollins, 1981.

———. *Where the Sidewalk Ends: The Poems & Drawings.* New York: HarperCollins, 1999.

Talking Like the Rain: A Read-To-Me Book of Poems. Boston: Little, Brown, 1992.

Tomie dePaola's Book of Poems. New York: Putnam, 1988.

Viorst, Judith. *The Alphabet from Z to A: (With Much Confusion on the Way).* New York: Atheneum, Maxwell Macmillan International, 1994.

Williams, Vera B. *Amber Was Brave, Essie Was Smart: The Story of Amber and Essie Told Here in Poems and Pictures.* New York: Greenwillow, 2001.

11

Weather or Not

THEME: Books with Weather Themes

PURPOSE: To interest students in using books to learn about the weather

MATERIALS:

Selection of fiction and nonfiction books that refer to forms of weather

Large cutout pictures of different types of weather

Two large sheets of poster board (yellow and white)

Weather stickers

STUDENT CONTRIBUTION:

Weather adages or sayings

Preparation for Book Event

TWO WEEKS BEFORE THE BOOK EVENT, send out an announcement inviting the staff and students.

> Mark Twain is reported to have said, "Everyone talks about the weather, but nobody does anything about it."
>
> Everyone is invited to come to our WEATHER OR NOT Book Event at the library to talk some more about it. There are lots of old adages or sayings about the weather, such as "Red sky at morning, sailors take warning. Red sky at night, sailors' delight." Please discuss weather sayings with your students, write down a few and send them to the library by the end of the week. We'll have fun with the weather, whether we do anything about it or not.

Using black markers on poster board, draw a large, smiling sun and a large puffy-faced wind and cut them out. Attach a strip of tag board to the back of each, forming a handle for a child to hold.

Gather fiction and nonfiction books about the weather from the library shelves.

Select some pictures of a variety of weather forms.

Collect weather adages from books, the Internet, and your memory. Here are a few suggestions.

- The daisy shuts its eye before rain.
- If smoke falls to the ground, it is likely to rain.
- If the wooly bear's brown stripe is wider than the black stripes, the winter will be long and hard.
- If March comes in like a lamb, it will go out like a lion. If it comes in like a lion, it will go out like a lamb.
- Rain before seven, clear by eleven.

Copy the following nursery rhyme onto tag board:

Whether the weather be fine
Or whether the weather be not,
Whether the weather be cold
Or whether the weather be hot,
We'll weather the weather
Whatever the weather,
Whether we like it or not!
Anonymous

A WEEK BEFORE THE BOOK EVENT, copy weather adages sent from the classrooms onto colored strips of paper, adding some of your own if necessary. Attach the adages to the bulletin board along with weather pictures and the verse. Add the caption WEATHER OR NOT.

Choose weather books to read aloud on the day of the event. Locate a copy of Aesop's fable, "The Wind and the Sun."

Select three students to help dramatize the fable with you and practice with them once. Two of them will hold the sun and wind posters in front of their bodies. The third child will dress as a traveler wearing a coat. They will act out the fable as you or a fellow staff member reads it.

Book Event Activity

Welcome staff and students to the activity and ask them to read the verse from the bulletin board with you. Discuss the meanings of the words "weather" and "whether." Thank them for the weather adages on the bulletin board and go over each one with the group.

Ask students to name different types of weather. Discuss which weather form they think is the strongest. Ask them whether they believe the sun or the wind is stronger.

Act out Aesop's fable, "The Wind and the Sun." Discuss the lesson learned from the fable.

Explore some fiction and nonfiction books about weather with the group. Include a copy of *The Farmer's Almanac* if possible, pointing out the sections on weather predictions. Encourage the students to read more about the weather.

Select one book from those shown and read it to the group.

End the activity by reading the weather verse together one last time.

Give each student a weather sticker as they leave.

Suggested Bibliography for Weather Theme

Primary Grades

Alexander, Lloyd. *How the Cat Swallowed Thunder.* New York: Dutton Children's Books, 2000.

Barrett, Judi. *Cloudy with a Chance of Meatballs.* New York: Aladdin Paperbacks, 1982.

Bourgoing, Pascale de. *Weather.* New York: Scholastic Books, 1989.

Branley, Franklyn Mansfield. *Down Comes the Rain.* New York: HarperCollins, 1997.

Cole, Joanna. *The Magic School Bus Inside a Hurricane.* New York: Scholastic Books, 1995.

Gibbons, Gail. *Weather Forecasting.* New York: Aladdin Paperbacks, 1987.

———. *Weather Words and What They Mean.* New York: Holiday House, 1990.

Hesse, Karen. *Come On, Rain!* New York: Scholastic Books, 1999.

Keats, Ezra Jack. *The Snowy Day.* New York: Viking, 1996.

Koscielniak, Bruce. *Geoffrey Groundhog Predicts the Weather.* Boston: Houghton Mifflin, 1995.

Martin, Bill. *Listen to the Rain.* New York: Henry Holt, 1988.

Munsch, Robert N. *Wait and See.* Toronto: Annick Press/Firefly, 1993.

Polacco, Patricia. *Thunder Cake.* New York: PaperStar, 1990.

Schulevitz, Uri. *Snow.* New York: Farrar, Straus and Giroux, 1998.

Singer, Marilyn. *On the Same Day in March: A Tour of the World's Weather.* New York: HarperCollins, 2000.

Spier, Peter. *Peter Spier's Rain.* New York: Bantam Doubleday Dell Books for Young Readers, 1997.

Stevenson, James. *Heat Wave at Mud Flat.* New York: Greenwillow Books, 1997.

Weigelt, Udo. *All-Weather Friends.* New York: North-South Books, 1999.

Zolotow, Charlotte. *When the Wind Stops.* New York: HarperCollins, 1995.

Intermediate Grades

Allaby, Michael. *DK Guide to Weather.* London and New York: DK, 2000.

Arnold, Caroline. *El Nino: Stormy Weather for People and Wildlife.* New York: Clarion Books, 1998.

Breen, Mark. *The Kids' Book of Weather Forecasting: Build a Weather Station, "Read" the Sky, & Make Predictions.* Charlotte, VT: Williamson Publishing, 2000.

Byars, Betsy Cromer. *Tornado.* New York: HarperCollins, 1996.

Christian, Spencer. *Can It Really Rain Frogs?: The World's Strangest Weather Events.* New York: John Wiley, 1997.

Davol, Marguerite W. *Why Butterflies Go by on Silent Wings.* New York: Orchard Books, 2001.

Farndon, John. *Weather.* New York: Benchmark Books, 2001.

Fleischman, Paul. *Lost!: A Story in String.* New York: Henry Holt, 2000.

Fleischman, Sid. *McBroom the Rainmaker.* New York: Price Stern Sloan, 1999, 1973.

Hiscock, Bruce. *The Big Storm.* New York: Atheneum, Maxwell Macmillan International, 1993.

Knight, Linsay. *Volcanoes & Earthquakes.* Alexandria, VA: Time-Life Books, 1995.

Lye, Keith. *Cold Climates.* Austin, TX: Raintree Steck-Vaughn, 1997.

The Old Farmer's Almanac. Dublin, NH: Yankee Publishing, 2002.

The Old Farmer's Almanac for Kids. Dublin, NH: Yankee Publishing, 2002.

Siebert, Patricia. *Discovering El Nino: How Fable and Fact Together Help Explain the Weather.* Brookfield, CT: Millbrook Press, 1999.

Simon, Seymour. *Weather.* New York: Morrow Junior Books, 1993.

Singer, Marilyn. *On the Same Day in March: A Tour of the World's Weather.* New York: HarperCollins, 2000.

Wyatt, Valerie. *Weather: FAQ, Frequently Asked Questions.* Toronto and Niagara Falls, NY: Kids Can Press, 2000.

12

Remembering Our Roots

THEME: Books about immigration and foreign countries

PURPOSE: To help students appreciate the diversity of America and to investigate their own ethnic heritages through literature

MATERIALS:

Selection of fiction and nonfiction books about Ellis Island, the Statue of Liberty, immigration, and various countries of the world

Posters of Ellis Island and the Statue of Liberty

A large outline of the United States for bulletin board

A large cutout of a tree including its roots

Tiny paper flags from countries of the world

STUDENT CONTRIBUTION:

Lists and symbols of their ethnic heritages

Preparation for Book Event

THREE WEEKS BEFORE THE BOOK EVENT, contact one or two persons from the school or community to speak for twenty minutes about their ethnic heritage. It could be someone fairly new to this country or simply someone with considerable cultural background knowledge. Select speakers who can relate their experiences to young people. Explain that they will be speaking to students of varying age levels and that it may be necessary to repeat their presentation to fit the schedule. Suggest that they may want to bring some items that reflect their own heritage. Ask them to allow for a question-and-answer time.

TWO WEEKS BEFORE THE BOOK EVENT, build interest in the event by sending out notices to staff and students.

> Join us in the library for a Book Event to celebrate our country's diversity by "Remembering Our Roots." The United States is a country of people of many different nationalities and races. Contributions from these varied backgrounds built our country and continue to make us strong. Please make a list of the cultural heritages in your class and send the list to the library by the end of this week. It is not necessary to list the students' names. Everyone is invited to wear or bring a symbol of his or her heritage to the Book Event. Come and help us celebrate our great country.

Using an overhead projector draw a large outline map of the United States and post it on the bulletin board. Cut out a large tree, including its root system and place in the middle of the map. Add large letters to spell REMEMBERING OUR ROOTS and pictures of Ellis Island or the Statue of Liberty, if available.

Create a display of fiction and nonfiction books pertaining to immigration, Ellis Island, the Statue of Liberty, and various nationalities of the world.

A WEEK BEFORE THE BOOK EVENT, contact the speakers again to remind them of the day and time.

Label the roots of the bulletin board tree with the nationalities submitted from the classrooms.

Select a theme-related book to read to each group.

ONE DAY BEFORE THE BOOK EVENT, remind the speakers one last time.

Book Event Activity

Wear something symbolic of the United States or of your own ethnic heritage. Welcome everyone and read a theme-related book. Appropriate choices might include *When Jessie Came Across the Sea* by Amy Hest or *Coming to America* by Eve Bunting.

Discuss the bulletin board and the concept of remembering our roots. Ask volunteers from the group about their ethnic heritages and inquire whether anyone is wearing symbols of his or her cultural background.

Introduce the speaker, and facilitate a question-and-answer period after the presentation. Lead the students in applause for the speaker.

Close the activity by reading the words written on the Statue of Liberty:

"Give me your tired, your poor,
Your huddled masses yearning to breathe free,

The wretched refuse of your teeming shore.
Send these, the homeless, tempest-tost to me.
I lift my lamp beside the golden door!"

Emma Lazarus, "The New Colossus"

Give each student a tiny paper flag to remember our country's roots.

Suggested Bibliography for Roots Theme

Primary Grades

Aliki. *Marianthe's Story. One, Painted Words; Marianthe's Story. Two. Spoken Memories.* New York: Greenwillow Books, 1998.

Bunting, Eve. *Dreaming of America: An Ellis Island Story.* Mahwah, NJ: Bridge Water Books, 2000.

———. *How Many Days to America?: A Thanksgiving Story.* New York: Clarion Books, 1988.

———. *A Picnic in October.* San Diego: Harcourt Brace, 1999.

Drummond, Allan. *Liberty!* New York: Farrar, Straus and Giroux, 2002.

Figueredo, D.H. *When This World Was New.* New York: Lee & Low Books, 1999.

Lawson, Robert. *They Were Strong and Good.* New York: Viking Press, 1966.

Levinson, Riki. *Watch the Stars Come Out.* New York: Penguin, 1995, 1985.

Maestro, Betsy. *Coming to America: The Story of Immigration.* New York: Scholastic Books, 1996.

———. *The Story of the Statue of Liberty.* New York: Mulberry, 1989, 1986.

Nagda, Ann Whitehead. *Dear Whiskers.* New York: Holiday House, 2000.

Polacco, Patricia. *The Keeping Quilt.* New York: Simon & Schuster Books for Young Readers, 1998.

Quiri, Patricia Ryon. *Ellis Island.* New York: Children's Press, 1998.

Ross, Alice. *The Copper Lady.* Minneapolis, MN: Carolrhoda Books, 1997.

Ross, Lillian Hammer. *Buba Leah and Her Paper Children.* Philadelphia: Jewish Publication Society, 1991.

Say, Allen. *Grandfather's Journey.* Boston: Houghton Mifflin, 1993.

Tarbescu, Edith. *Annushka's Voyage.* New York: Clarion Books, 1998.

Wells, Rosemary. *Streets of Gold.* New York: Dial Books for Young Readers, 1999.

Intermediate Grades

Avi. *Beyond the Western Sea. Book II, Lord Kirkle's Money.* New York: Avon Camelot, 1998.

Bartoletti, Susan Campbell. *A Coal Miner's Bride: The Diary of Anetka Kaminska.* New York: Scholastic Books, 2000.

Cohen, Barbara. *Molly's Pilgrim.* New York: Lothrop, Lee & Shepard Books, 1998.

Curlee, Lynn. *Liberty.* New York: Atheneum Books for Young Readers, 2000.

Doherty, Craig A. *The Statue of Liberty.* Woodbridge, CT: Blackbirch Press, 1997.

Freedman, Russell. *Immigrant Kids.* New York: Puffin Books, 1995.

Graff, Nancy Price. *Where the River Runs: A Portrait of a Refugee Family.* Boston: Little, Brown, 1993.

Grenquist, Barbara. *Recent American Immigrants: Cubans.* New York: Franklin Watts, 1991. (And other titles from the Recent American Immigrants series.)

Gundisch, Karin. *How I Became an American.* Chicago: Cricket Books, 2001.

Hesse, Karen. *Letters from Rifka.* New York: Henry Holt, 1992.

Hest, Amy. *When Jessie Came Across the Sea.* Cambridge, MA: Candlewick Press, 1997.

Hoobler, Dorothy and Thomas Hoobler. *The Italian American Family Album.* New York: Oxford University Press, 1994. (And other titles from the American Family Albums series.)

I Was Dreaming To Come to America: Memories from the Ellis Island Oral History Project. New York: Viking, 1995.

Jacobs, William Jay. *Ellis Island: New Hope in a New Land.* New York: Atheneum Books for Young Readers, 1990.

Mayerson, Evelyn Wilde. *The Cat Who Escaped from Steerage: A Bubbemeiser.* New York: Atheneum Books for Young Readers, 1990.

Olson, Kay Melchisedech. *Chinese Immigrants: 1850–1900.* Mankato, MN: Blue Earth Books, 2002. (And other Coming to America titles from this series.)

Shaw, Janet Beeler. *Meet Kirsten: An American Girl.* Middleton, WI: Pleasant Company, 1986.

Woodruff, Elvira. *The Memory Coat.* New York: Scholastic Books, 1999.

———. *The Orphan of Ellis Island: A Time-Travel Adventure.* New York: Scholastic Books, 1997.

13

It's How You Play the Game

THEME: Recreational and Professional Sports

PURPOSE: Motivate students to read, emphasizing their interest in sports

MATERIALS:

Selection of books and magazines about recreational sports, professional sports, and athletes

Sports-related bookmark or pencil eraser for each student

STUDENT CONTRIBUTION:

A cutout drawing of a sports participant or a professional sports team logo

Preparation for Book Event

TWO WEEKS BEFORE THE BOOK EVENT, send out the invitation to staff and students.

> Please come to an "It's How You Play the Game" Book Event at the library. We are going to celebrate favorite sporting activities. We'll include a wide range of sports from recreational activities such as hiking and sledding to favorite professional sports such as major league baseball or even the Olympics. We invite students to draw, color, and cut out either an athlete enjoying a favorite sport (e.g., a swimmer, a ball player, a biker) or a logo of a favorite professional team. We encourage them to represent a wide range of sports from any season of the year. Students should use large (at least twelve inches by fourteen inches) sheets of drawing paper so others can appreciate their work. Please send the drawings to the library by the end of this week. Everyone is encouraged to wear T-shirts or caps representing favorite sporting activities or teams to the Book Event. Let's enjoy the games together.

Arrange a display of both fiction and nonfiction books pertaining to a wide range of recreational and professional sporting activities.

Locate a copy of Abbott and Costello's comedy routine, "Who's on First?" as performed in *The Naughty Nineties* (1945). Select two students or staff members to read it aloud during the Book Event to the intermediate grades.

Cut out large bulletin board letters to spell the words IT'S HOW YOU PLAY THE GAME. Make smaller signs for each of the major sports—basketball, football, baseball, soccer, etc.

Purchase sports-related bookmarks or pencil erasers.

A WEEK BEFORE THE BOOK EVENT, separate the student drawings according to the sport. Divide the bulletin board into sections for each sport. Put up some large construction paper cutouts to represent backgrounds such as fields, trees, or water. Backgrounds will depend upon the sports to be represented. Arrange the figures and logos drawn by students in the appropriate settings on the board. Add some cutouts from sports magazines if necessary to balance and complete the arrangement. Display some sports uniforms around the room if available.

Rehearse the reading of "Who's on First?" with volunteers.

Read through the grades K–3 responsive reading as printed in the next section of this chapter.

Select picture books to read to each group.

Book Event Activity

Dress casually, wearing a sports T-shirt or cap to welcome everyone to the activity. Read them the old adage attributed to sportswriter Grantland Rice, "It matters not if you win or lose, it's how you play the game." Ask the students to explain what the saying means to them. Discuss the drawings on the bulletin board and recommend some books that they might enjoy. Comment on the sports shirts and caps they have worn.

Grades K–3: Explain that you are going to read them a short story about a boy named Charlie who loved all kinds of sports. They are to help you with the story. When they hear certain words, they are to respond as follows:

Sports	Clap hands
Football	"Touchdown!"
Basketball	"Swish!"
Soccer	"Score!"
Baseball	"St-ri-ke!"
Race car	"Vroom!"
Golf	"Fore!"
Bike	Make steering motion with hands

Practice the responses with them a few times. Then read the story, pausing after each italicized word to allow time for a response.

Charlie Loves *Sports*

Once there was a little boy named Charlie. He loved his family and his big black dog. He especially liked strawberry ice cream and corn on the cob. He enjoyed reading books and watching television. But most of all he really liked *sports*. He liked all kinds of *sports*. He liked *football*. He liked *basketball*. He liked *soccer*. He liked *baseball*. He even liked watching *race cars* and people playing *golf*. His parents asked him to name his favorite *sport*, but Charlie couldn't decide which one he really liked best.

One day Charlie asked his mother for permission to go to the library to look for books on *sports*. Maybe then he could decide on his favorite and learn all about it. Charlie's mother said, "Yes," and he jumped on his *bike* and pedaled off to the library. He looked through a lot of the books on the shelves. He found one that explained how to play *soccer*. He found another that told the story of a famous *baseball* player. Another book had a picture of a *race car* on the cover. There was a big book about his favorite *basketball* team. There were books about *football* and even about *golf*. Charlie looked at every book. Which *sport* was his favorite? He still liked them all. Then he saw one last book. It was called, *Ev-*

erything You Ever Wanted To Know about Sports and More Besides. What a great book! It had all his favorites: *baseball, football, soccer, golf, and basketball.* It even had parts on *race cars* and riding a *bike.* What more could he ask? Charlie signed the book out, jumped on his *bike,* and pedaled home to read about his favorite thing: *sports!*

Grades 4–6: Perform the skit, "Who's on First?"

Both groups: Read a short book to them about sports. Give each student a sports-related bookmark or pencil eraser to commemorate the event.

Suggested Bibliography for Sports Theme

Primary Grades

Adler, David A. *The Babe & I.* San Diego: Harcourt Brace, 1999.

Armstrong, Kristin. *Lance Armstrong: The Race of His Life.* New York: Grosset & Dunlap, 2000.

Brown, Marc Tolon. *D.W. Rides Again!* Boston: Little, Brown, 1993.

Bruchac, Joseph. *The Great Ball Game: A Muskogee Story.* New York: Dial Books for Young Readers, 1994.

Dubois, Muriel L. *I Like Sports: What Can I Be?* Mankato, MN: Bridgestone Books, 2000.

Gibbons, Gail. *My Baseball Book.* New York: HarperCollins, 2000.

Haskins, James. *Champion: The Story of Muhammad Ali.* New York: Walker, 2002.

Isadora, Rachel. *Sophie Skates.* New York: Putnam, 1999.

Kennedy, X.J. *Elympics.* New York: Philomel Books, 1999.

Kessler, Leonard P. *Kick, Pass, and Run.* New York: HarperCollins, 1996.

Kraus, Robert. *Mort the Sport.* New York: Orchard Books, 2000.

Krensky, Stephen. *Arthur Makes the Team.* Boston: Little, Brown, 1998.

LaMarche, Jim. *The Raft.* New York: HarperCollins, 2000.

London, Jonathan. *White Water.* New York: Viking, 2001.

Parish, Peggy. *Play Ball, Amelia Bedelia.* New York: HarperCollins, 1996.

Rappaport, Doreen. *Dirt on Their Skirts: The Story of the Young Women Who Won the World Championship.* New York: Dial Books for Young Readers, 2000.

Rey, H.A. *Curious George Rides a Bike.* Boston: Houghton Mifflin, 1993.

Sampson, Michael R. *The Football That Won.* New York: Henry Holt, 1996.

Sports! Sports! Sports!: A Poetry Collection. New York: HarperCollins, 1999.

Intermediate Grades

Arnosky, Jim. *Freshwater Fish & Fishing.* New York: Four Winds Press, 1982.

Blake, Robert J. *Akiak: A Tale from the Iditarod.* New York: Philomel Books, 1997.

Bledsoe, Lucy Jane. *The Big Bike Race.* New York: Holiday House, 1995.

———. *Hoop Girlz.* New York: Holiday House, 2002.

Christopher, Matt. *Dirt Bike Racer.* Boston: Little, Brown, 1979.

———. *Great Moments in Baseball History.* Boston: Little, Brown, 1996.

Ethan, Eric. *Daytona 500.* Milwaukee, WI: Gareth Stevens, 1999.

Gardner, Robert. *Experimenting with Science in Sports.* New York: Franklin Watts, 1993.

Gordon, John. *The Kids Book of Golf.* Tonawanda, NY: Kids Can Press, 2001.

The Greatest Baseball Stories Ever Told. Guilford, CT: Lyons Press, 2001.

Gutman, Bill. *Brett Favre: Leader of the Pack.* Brookfield, CT: Millbrook Press, 1998. (And other titles from the Millbrook Sports World Series.)

Hoyt-Goldsmith, Diane. *Lacrosse: The National Game of the Iroquois.* New York: Holiday House, 1998.

Hughes, Dean. *Home Run Hero.* New York: Atheneum, 1999.

Kauchak, Therese. *Good Sports: Winning, Losing, and Everything in Between.* Middleton, WI: Pleasant Company, 1999.

Konigsburg, E.L. *About the B'nai Bagels.* New York: Atheneum, 1970.

Macy, Sue. *A Whole New Ball Game.* New York: Henry Holt, 1993.

Osborn, Kevin. *Scholastic Encyclopedia of Sports in the United States.* New York: Scholastic Books, 1997.

Owens, Thomas S. *Collecting Baseball Memorabilia.* Brookfield, CT: Millbrook Press, 1996.

Park, Barbara. *Skinnybones.* New York: Random House, 1997.

Savage, Jeff. *Motocross Cycles.* Mankato, MN: Capstone Press, 1996.

Slote, Alfred. *The Trading Game.* New York: HarperTrophy, 1992.

Spinelli, Jerry. *There's a Girl in My Hammerlock.* New York: Aladdin Paperbacks, 1993.

Sports Illustrated for Kids magazine. New York: Time.

Sullivan, George. *All about Hockey.* New York: Putnam, 1998.

Thayer, Ernest Lawrence. *Casey at the Bat: A Ballad of the Republic Sung in the Year 1888.* Brooklyn, NY: Handprint Books, 2000.

Tunis, John Roberts. *The Kid from Tomkinsville.* San Diego: Harcourt Brace, 1987.

14

Save Our Earth

THEME: Fiction and nonfiction books about conserving the Earth's resources

PURPOSE: To develop student awareness of library resources and their use in researching conservation topics

MATERIALS:

A display of fiction and nonfiction books and periodicals related to stewardship of land, air, water, and wildlife resources

Posters or large pictures of landforms, waterways, and wildlife

A large colored cutout of the Earth

Cutouts of puffy clouds, stars, and comet tails

Wildlife bookmarks for the students

Preparation for Book Event

TWO WEEKS BEFORE THE BOOK EVENT, send out a notice to staff and students.

> Every day we are using up and polluting Earth's resources—its land, water, air, and wildlife. Please help us think of ways to "Save the Earth" and share your ideas at our next Book Event. We hope you will discuss conservation in your class and make up several slogans about this topic. Ideas may be as simple as "recycle soda cans" or as complex as "generate electricity with wind power." A special display of books on conservation is available in the library. Please send your slogans to the library by the end of this week. Everyone is invited to bring loose change to this Book Event to contribute toward rescuing an endangered animal. Come and learn about it!

Locate books on conservation and arrange a display for student research.

Arrange with the teacher of an intermediate class to have a group of students draw, color, and cut out figures and objects to illustrate *The Lorax* by Dr. Seuss. Explain that you will read the story while the students place their drawings on a freestanding bulletin board.

Cut out a large Earth from blue paper and lightly sketch continent lines upon it. Cut out puffy white clouds, colorful stars, and comet tails that are large enough to contain the students' slogans.

Search wildlife adoption possibilities online or through catalogs from wildlife conservation groups. These groups offer programs for students to "adopt" an endangered animal by sending a small donation and receiving a sponsorship certificate in return.

Locate a stuffed animal to represent the species selected.

Purchase wildlife bookmarks.

A WEEK BEFORE THE BOOK EVENT, assemble the bulletin board, adding the conservation slogans to the clouds and comet tails. Add nature pictures to the borders of the display.

Select conservation-related books and poems to be read at the Event.

Decorate a large jar for collecting the coins.

Remind students to bring loose change to the event to adopt an endangered animal.

Practice several times with the students helping to illustrate *The Lorax* as you read the story.

Book Event Activity

Place the coin jar and stuffed animal so that staff and students can drop loose change into the container as they arrive. Welcome the students, wearing a conservation or animal theme T-shirt.

Read a poem about the animal species to be adopted. Read an excerpt about the animal from a nature field guide. Discuss the plight of the animal and its fight for survival. Thank everyone for the contributions and explain the adoption process.

Discuss the bulletin board and the conservation slogans. Display the resource books to encourage more research on the topic. Encourage students to express their own ideas about conservation in general.

Play "Good News–Bad News" with the group, using conservation themes. Give the group a Good News–Bad News example and then have them continue responses. Segments should be brief, ending on a positive note.

Example 1

Good News: I bought a can of soda.

Bad News: I threw the empty can on the side of the road.

Good News: Etc.

Example 2

Good News: We saw a baby seal on the beach.

Bad News: Its mother was gone.

Good News: Etc.

Example 3

Good News: There's a new factory in town.

Bad News: They're polluting the air.

Good News: Etc.

Read the story of *The Lorax* by Dr. Seuss as the selected students place their characters and objects on a freestanding bulletin board. Discuss the meaning of the story briefly. Thank the students involved.

Close the activity by sending students on their way with wildlife bookmarks.

Suggested Bibliography for Conservation Theme

Primary Grades

Atwell, Debby. *River.* Boston: Houghton Mifflin, 1999.

Bang, Molly. *Common Ground: The Water, Earth, and Air We Share.* New York: Blue Sky Press, 1997.

Berenstain, Stan. *The Berenstain Bears Don't Pollute (Anymore).* New York: Random House, 1991.

Breiter, Herta S. *Pollution.* Austin, TX: Steck-Vaughn, 1991.

Bunting, Eve. *Someday a Tree.* New York: Clarion, 1993.

Cherry, Lynne. *The Great Kapok Tree: A Tale of the Amazon Rain Forest.* San Diego: Harcourt Brace, 1990.

Collard, Sneed B. *Butterfly Count.* New York: Holiday House, 2002.

Dobson, David. *Can We Save Them?: Endangered Species of North America.* Watertown, MA: Charlesbridge, 1997.

Fleming, Denise. *Where Once There Was a Wood.* New York: Henry Holt, 1996.

Gibbons, Gail. *Sea Turtles.* New York: Holiday House, 1995.

Guiberson, Brenda Z. *Into the Sea.* New York: Henry Holt, 1996.

Hendrick, Mary Jean. *If Anything Ever Goes Wrong at the Zoo.* San Diego: Harcourt Brace, 1996.

McCully, Emily Arnold. *Hurry!* San Diego: Browndeer Press/Harcourt, 2000.

Peet, Bill. *Farewell to Shady Glade.* Boston: Houghton Mifflin, 1994.

Ray, Mary Lyn. *Pumpkins: A Story for a Field.* San Diego: Harcourt Brace Jovanovich, 1992.

Ross, Kathy. *Every Day Is Earth Day: A Craft Book.* Brookfield, CT: Millbrook Press, 1995.

Seuss, Dr. *The Lorax.* New York: Random House, 1971.

Van Allsburg, Chris. *Just a Dream.* Boston: Houghton Mifflin, 1990.

Intermediate Grades

Arnosky, Jim. *Arnosky's Ark.* Washington, DC: National Geographic Society, 1999.

Asimov, Isaac. *Where Does Garbage Go?* Milwaukee: Gareth Stevens Children's Books, 1992.

Brown, Ruth. *The World That Jack Built.* New York: Dutton, 1991.

Cerullo, Mary M. *Coral Reef: A City That Never Sleeps.* New York: Cobblehill Books, 1996.

Cherry, Lynne. *A River Ran Wild: An Environmental History.* San Diego: Harcourt Brace, 1992.

Gibbons, Gail. *Nature's Green Umbrella: Tropical Rain Forests.* New York: Morrow Junior Books, 1994.

Greenaway, Theresa. *Whales.* Austin, TX: Raintree Steck-Vaughn, 2001.

Hooper, Meredith. *The Drop in My Drink: The Story of Water on Our Planet.* New York: Viking, 1998.

Lasky, Kathryn. *Interrupted Journey: Saving Endangered Sea Turtles.* Cambridge, MA: Candlewick, 2001.

Macaulay, David. *Angelo.* Boston: Houghton Mifflin, 2002.

Mitchell, Joyce Slayton. *Crashed, Smashed, and Mashed: A Trip to Junkyard Heaven.* Berkeley, CA: Tricycle Press, 2001.

Patent, Dorothy Hinshaw. *Eagles of America.* New York: Holiday House, 1995.

———. *Gray Wolf, Red Wolf.* New York: Clarion Books, 1990.

Pringle, Laurence P. *Global Warming: The Threat of Earth's Changing Climate.* New York: SeaStar Books, 2001.

Seuss, Dr. *The Lorax.* New York: Random House, 1971.

Taylor, J. David. *Endangered Forest Animals.* New York: Crabtree, 1991.

Thomas, Peggy. *Marine Mammal Preservation.* Brookfield, CT: Twenty-First Century Books, 2000.

Walker, Sally M. *Rhinos.* Minneapolis: Carolrhoda Books, 1996.

15

Questions and Answers: The Library Challenge

THEME: Library Resources

PURPOSE: To excite students about finding answers by using library resources

MATERIALS:

- Selection of reference books (atlas, encyclopedia, dictionary, almanac, thesaurus, yearbook, periodical guide, telephone directory)
- Posters on Dewey decimal system, online catalog use, and library references
- Colorful book jackets from familiar titles
- Questions for Library Challenge
- Play money
- Microphone (real or toy)
- Play money bookmarks for each student (available in library catalogs)

STUDENT CONTRIBUTION:

Five questions and answers and participation in the Library Challenge

Preparation for Book Event

THREE WEEKS BEFORE THE BOOK EVENT, send out the invitation.

Everyone is invited to attend the Library Challenge Book Event! We will have fun answering questions in a game-show format. Questions will range from simple to challenging and will cover authors, titles, and use of library resources. Please ask your class to make up five questions that can be answered by using the library and sources such as a nonfiction book, a dictionary, an encyclopedia, an atlas, a thesaurus, or other reference book. Include the correct answer and cite the source for the answer. Enclosed is a bibliography listing reference books and topic-related books that are available on the reserve shelf in the library for student and teacher use. Please send the questions and answers to the library by the end of this week. Also please send the names of two students from your class who are ready and willing to accept the challenge of being a contestant. Come and enjoy the fun!

Locate or make posters for a bulletin board on the Dewey decimal system, online catalog use, and library references.

Set up a reserve section of reference materials and topic-related books. Compile a bibliography of these materials and send to teachers with the invitation.

TWO WEEKS BEFORE THE BOOK EVENT, make up a variety of age-appropriate questions for the Challenge game. Include the contributions from the classes. Place them into three categories according to degree of difficulty (1 = easy, 2 = medium, 3 = challenging). Twenty questions at each level are sufficient for the Book Event itself, but more will be necessary if students want to follow up with questions after the event. Type the questions onto sheets of paper and make copies for each class for follow-up activities after the event. Use one copy to make an answer key for yourself. Laminate one copy and cut the questions apart. Sort them into three containers labeled 1, 2, and 3.

Sample First-Round Questions

1 What is the paper cover that protects the book? (jacket)

1 What do we call the person who writes a book? (author)

1 What lists the order of the chapters and their pages in the front of a book? (table of contents)

1 Who had a "terrible, horrible, no-good, very bad day"? (Alexander)

2 What do we call the time and place a story happens? (setting)

2 Where is the listing of all available books in the library? (online catalog)

2 What date shows the year a book is published? (copyright date)

2 What reference book contains many maps? (atlas)

3 Name the system by which nonfiction books are arranged on the shelves. (Dewey decimal system)

3 How are fiction books arranged on the shelves? (by author's last name)

3 What do we call a book about a real person's life, written by that same person? (autobiography)

3 What was Dr. Seuss's real name? (Theodor Geisel)

Sample Second-Round Questions

(Students may answer or explain what resource they would use to find the answer.)

1 What is the plural form of the word "ox?" (oxen—dictionary)

1 What is a baby kangaroo called? (joey—encyclopedia, dictionary)

1 In what continent is France? (Europe—atlas, encyclopedia)

1 In what reference book could you find your friend's address? (telephone directory)

2 What is the capitol of New York? (Albany—atlas, encyclopedia)

2 Who invented the telephone? (Bell—encyclopedia)

2 What body of water is west of Florida? (Gulf of Mexico—atlas, encyclopedia)

2 Name a synonym for "skid." (slip, slide—dictionary, thesaurus)

3 What is the longest river in the world? (Nile—almanac, encyclopedia)

3 What colors are in the flag of Italy? (green, white, red—almanac, encyclopedia)

3 Who won the first World Series baseball game? (Chicago—almanac, encyclopedia)

3 Who is quoted as saying, "A thing of beauty is a joy forever?" (Keats—*Bartlett's Familiar Quotations*)

3 What is a synonym for "frugality?" (thriftiness, economy—thesaurus, dictionary)

A WEEK BEFORE THE BOOK EVENT, arrange the bulletin board display. Use posters, familiar book jackets, large dollar signs, play money, and the words: ANSWER THE LIBRARY CHALLENGE.

Check to be sure you have two volunteer contestants from each class.

Locate or make a table microphone for stage set. Make a small stand-up sign that reads LIBRARY CHALLENGE.

Make a copy of the Library Challenge game directions.

Library Challenge Game Directions

Welcome to the LIBRARY CHALLENGE—the game that tests your ability to use your library to answer all of your questions! Today we will see who is able to meet this challenge! When I call your name, come to the stage and be seated. I will ask you three questions. If you answer them correctly, you will receive huge amounts in paper bills! If you miss one question, you will receive one more chance. If you miss two questions, it will be someone else's turn to meet the Library Challenge. Our first contestant is

______________________________.

Make a simple chart with spaces for student names and correct responses for a follow-up activity of researching questions on their own.

Arrange a display of reference books and titles from the bibliographies at the end of this chapter.

Book Event Activity

Set up a table with the microphone, question containers, sign, play money, and chairs for the emcee and one contestant. Set up a research table in the corner of the room with reference materials. Ask one of the adults to supervise the table during the game show. Dress up as the emcee for the occasion.

Greet everyone as the game show emcee. Explain that there will be a little warm-up before the game. Discuss the bulletin board posters and the display of reference books. Ask students why they would use specific reference books.

Read the Library Challenge directions to the group and proceed with the game. Ask category 1 and 2 questions with the primary grades. Use all three categories of questions for the intermediate grades. Begin with one of the first-round questions that require a specific answer. Reward students flamboyantly with paper money when they are correct. Announce correct answers if they miss. Then progress to the second-level questions and accept either the specific response or an explanation of what resource would be used to find the correct answer. If they give the latter, challenge them to leave the stage to use the resource and locate the answer before the end of the Book Event. When someone has missed two questions or leaves to research an answer, move quickly to the next contestant. When all original contestants have had an opportunity, open up the game to volunteers from the group. Near the close of the program, allow those contestants who have been researching questions time to reveal their answers. Announce that more questions will be available for research during the next few weeks. Challenge students to submit their answers. Show them the chart that will record student names and number of correct answers. Give teachers a copy of the research questions. Suggest that students read some of the displayed books about authors, resources, and challenges. Give all students a play money bookmark as they leave.

Suggested Bibliography for Challenge Theme

Primary Grades

Aliki, *How a Book Is Made.* New York: HarperCollins, 1986.

Cole, Joanna. *On the Bus with Joanna Cole: A Creative Autobiography.* Portsmouth, NH: Heinemann, 1996.

Deedy, Carmen Agra. *The Library Dragon.* Atlanta: Peachtree, 1994.

Gibbons, Gail. *Check It Out!: The Book about Libraries.* San Diego: Harcourt Brace, 1985.

Holub, Joan. *Why Do Cats Meow?* New York: Dial Books for Young Readers, 2001.

———. *Why Do Dogs Bark?* New York: Dial Books for Young Readers, 2001.

Lester, Helen. *Author: A True Story.* Boston: Houghton Mifflin, 1997.

MacLeod, Elizabeth. *What Did Dinosaurs Eat?: And Other Things You Want To Know about Dinosaurs.* Tonawanda, NY: Kids Can Press, 2001.

Miller, Margaret. *Who Uses This?* New York: Greenwillow Books, 1990.

Muth, Jon J. *The Three Questions.* New York: Scholastic Books, 2002.

Polacco, Patricia. *Firetalking.* Katonah, NY: R.C. Owen, 1994. (And other *Meet the Author* titles from this series.)

Ripley, Catherine. *Why?: The Best Ever Question and Answer Book about Nature, Science and the World Around You.* New York: Firefly Books, 2001.

Stevens, Janet. *From Pictures to Words: A Book about Making a Book.* New York: Holiday House, 1995.

VanCleave, Janice Pratt. *Janice VanCleave's Play and Find Out about Bugs: Easy Experiments for Young Children.* New York: John Wiley, 1999.

Walsh, Melanie. *Do Donkeys Dance?* Boston: Houghton Mifflin, 2000.

Young, Ruth. *Who Says Moo?* New York: Viking, 1994.

Resources such as a simple dictionary, telephone directory, atlas, and encyclopedia.

INTERMEDIATE GRADES

Alexander, Sally Hobart. *Do You Remember the Color Blue?: And Other Questions Kids Ask about Blindness.* New York: Viking, 2000.

Author Talk: Conversations with Judy Blume...et al. New York: Simon & Schuster Books for Young Readers, 2000.

Cleary, Beverly. *Dear Mr. Henshaw.* New York: Morrow Junior Books, 1983.

Clements, Andrew. *Frindle.* New York: Simon & Schuster Books for Young Readers, 1996.

De Paola, Tomie. *On My Way.* New York: Putnam, 2001.

Fertl, Dagmar. *Bears.* New York: Sterling, 2000.

Flanagan, Alice K. *Exploring the Library.* Milwaukee, WI: Gareth Stevens, 2001.

Hildick, E.W. *The Serial Sneak Thief.* New York: Cavendish, 1997.

Konigsburg, E.L. *The View from Saturday.* New York: Atheneum Books for Young Readers, 1996.

Learning Works Meet the Author Series. Santa Barbara, CA: Learning Works, 1997.

Marcus, Leonard S. *Side by Side: Five Favorite Picture Book Teams Go To Work.* New York: Walker & Company, 2001.

Myers, Jack. *Scientists Probe 11 Animal Mysteries: On the Trail of the Komodo Dragon and Other Explorations of Science in Action.* Honesdale, PA: Caroline House/Boyds Mills Press, 1999.

Peet, Bill. *Bill Peet: An Autobiography.* Boston: Houghton Mifflin, 1989.

Siberell, Anne. *Bravo? Brava? A Night at the Opera: Behind the Scenes with Composers, Cast, and Crew.* New York: Oxford University Press, 2001.

Wyatt, Valerie. *Weather: FAQ, Frequently Asked Questions.* Niagara Falls, NY: Kids Can Press, 2000.

Resources such as atlas, encyclopedia, dictionary, almanac, thesaurus, quotation resource, periodical guide, telephone directory.

16

The Moral of the Story

THEME: Fables

PURPOSE: Introduce students to fables and the lessons they teach

MATERIALS:

Selection of fables for display

Copies of well-known fables and a listing of their main characters, one for each class

Matching worksheet of fable titles to the morals of the stories

STUDENT CONTRIBUTION:

A cutout drawing of fable characters

Preparation for Book Event

TWO WEEKS BEFORE THE BOOK EVENT, send out the invitation to staff and students.

You are invited to learn about "The Moral of the Story" at our Fable Book Event coming soon to the library. We will have fun reading fables and discussing the lessons they teach. Please ask some students in your class to draw, color, and cut out figures for the main characters of the fable enclosed with this invitation. Students should use large (twelve inches by eighteen inches) sheets of drawing paper so others can appreciate their work. Size relationships should be taken into consideration if possible. For instance, characters such as mice should be drawn smaller than lions. Please send the drawings to the library by the end of this week. If a few students in your class would like to dramatize your fable at the Book Event, please let me know. Come and meet a man named Aesop.

Include a copy of a fable and a listing of its main characters with the invitation. Each class should receive a different title and list.

Arrange a display of books containing fables in a special area.

Cut out large bulletin board letters to spell the words THE MORAL OF THE STORY. Print the morals of the fables given to the classrooms on colored paper in large type. Make a curving walkway for the bulletin board upon which to place the fable characters drawn by the students.

Determine which classes would like to perform a simple dramatization of their fable at the Book Event.

Make up a matching worksheet of fable titles and morals. Include the fables illustrated by the classes, but also add more to encourage further reading. Run off copies to give to all students at the Book Event.

A WEEK BEFORE THE BOOK EVENT, design the bulletin board by arranging the fable characters in groups according to their fable along the walkway. Place the papers with the morals along the sides or bottom of the bulletin board. Add one paper listing all the fable titles. Add the large letters to spell THE MORAL OF THE STORY.

Select fables to read to each group.

Research the story of Aesop in an encyclopedia or online for background understanding.

Make a simple Greek toga costume by sewing up a white sheet, adding a rope belt, and wearing sandals. Use iron-on black letters to spell AESOP on the toga.

Book Event Activity

Dress in the Aesop costume and greet the students formally. Introduce yourself as a Greek slave who lived more than 2,000 years ago in the seventh or sixth century B.C. Explain that you loved to tell stories and that you were freed because you told them well. Even kings asked you to help them because they felt you were wise. Although some people believe you were just a legend, Greek historians wrote about you, and your stories were written down about 200 years after you died. Explain that not all fables were written by you and that many other authors have written fables also. However, it is believed that you were responsible for many of the most well known fables.

Explain that fables were short stories usually told by one person to another, and they were often about animals. The stories were told to teach lessons of good, bad, wise, and foolish behavior. At first fables were intended for adults, but because they were about animals they came to be considered children's stories.

Read a fable to the group and discuss the moral with them.

Discuss the bulletin board characters by asking each class to identify their characters and the title of their fable. Ask students to match the correct moral to the fable.

Discuss rules of being a good audience and invite any classes that have prepared a dramatization of their fable to perform.

If time permits, read a final fable to the group. Give students a fable worksheet and encourage them to read further fables.

Match the Moral to the Story Worksheet

Directions: Match the number of the moral to its correct fable.

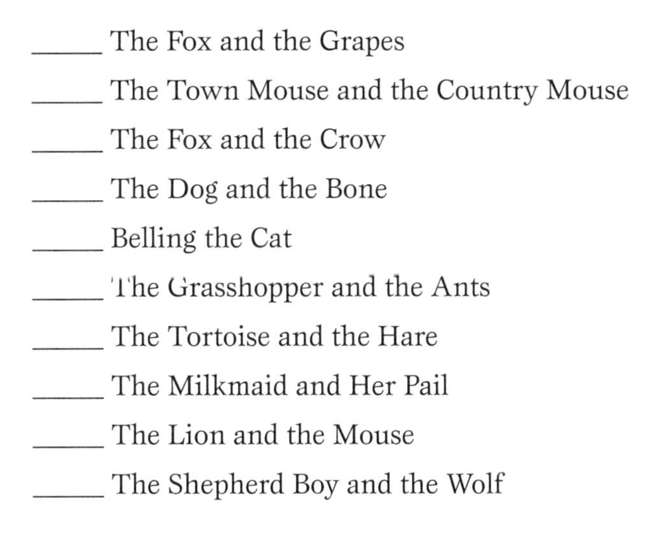

_____ The Fox and the Grapes

_____ The Town Mouse and the Country Mouse

_____ The Fox and the Crow

_____ The Dog and the Bone

_____ Belling the Cat

_____ The Grasshopper and the Ants

_____ The Tortoise and the Hare

_____ The Milkmaid and Her Pail

_____ The Lion and the Mouse

_____ The Shepherd Boy and the Wolf

1. Slow and steady wins the race.
2. Don't give up what's real for what isn't.
3. Nobody believes a liar even when he tells the truth.
4. A crust of bread in peace is better than a feast in fear.
5. Don't put off until tomorrow what you should do today.
6. Even the humblest friend may be of great help.
7. It's easier to suggest a plan than to carry it out.
8. Never trust a flatterer.
9. Don't count your chickens before they're hatched.
10. It's easy to scorn what you cannot get.

Answers: 10, 4, 8, 2, 7, 5, 1, 9, 6, 3

Suggested Bibliography for Fable Theme

Primary Grades

Brett, Jan. *Town Mouse, Country Mouse.* New York: Putnam, 1994.

Climo, Shirley. *The Little Red Ant and the Great Big Crumb: A Mexican Fable.* New York: Clarion Books, 1995.

Cooney, Barbara. *Chanticleer and the Fox.* New York: HarperCollins, 1989.

Cuyler, Margery. *Roadsigns: A Harey Race with a Tortoise: An Aesop Fable.* Delray Beach, FL: Winslow Press, 2000.

Dahlie, Elizabeth. *Bernelly & Harriet: The Country Mouse and the City Mouse.* Boston: Little, Brown, 2002.

Floyd, Lucy. *Rabbit and Turtle Go to School.* San Diego: Harcourt, 2000.

Goodall, Jane. *The Eagle & the Wren.* New York: North-South Books, 2000.

McAllister, Angela. *Barkus, Sly and the Golden Egg.* New York: Bloomsbury Children's Books, 2002.

Meserve, Adria. *Smog the City Dog.* San Francisco: Chronicle Books, 2002.

Poole, Amy Lowry. *The Ant and the Grasshopper.* New York: Holiday House, 2000.

Potter, Beatrix. *Tale of Johnny Town-Mouse.* New York and London: F. Warne, 1987.

Sykes, Julie. *That's Not Fair, Hare!* Haupauge, NY: Barron's Educational Series, 2001.

Stevens, Janet. *The Tortoise and the Hare: An Aesop Fable.* New York: Holiday House, 1984.

Ward, Helen. *The Hare and the Tortoise: A Fable from Aesop.* Brookfield, CT: Millbrook Press, 1999.

Young, Ed. *Seven Blind Mice.* New York: Philomel Books, 1992.

Intermediate Grades

Banks, Lynne Reid. *The Adventures of King Midas.* New York: Avon, 1993.

Carle, Eric. *Eric Carle's Treasury of Classic Stories for Children.* New York: Scholastic Books, 1988.

Classic Treasury of Aesop's Fables. Philadelphia: Running Press, 1999.

Fables from Aesop. New York: Viking, 2000.

Fox, Mem. *Feathers and Fools.* San Diego: Harcourt Brace, 1996.

Hamilton, Virginia. *A Ring of Tricksters: Animal Tales from North America, the West Indies, and Africa.* New York: Blue Sky Press, 1997.

Hartman, Bob. *The Wolf Who Cried Boy.* New York: Putnam, 2002.

Johnston, Tony. *The Cowboy and the Black-eyed Pea.* New York: Putnam & Grosset Group, 1996.

Linzer, Lila. *Once Upon an Island.* Asheville, NC: Front Street, 1998.

Lobel, Arnold. *Fables.* New York: HarperCollins, 1980

Pinkney, Jerry. *Aesop's Fables.* New York: SeaStar Books, 2000.

Scieszka, Jon. *Squids Will Be Squids: Fresh Morals, Beastly Fables.* New York: Viking, 1998.

Silverstein, Shel. *The Missing Piece Meets the Big O.* New York: Harper & Row, 2000.

A Treasury of Children's Literature. Boston: Houghton Mifflin, 1992.

Watts, Bernadette. *The Rich Man and the Shoemaker: A Fable by La Fontaine.* New York: North-South Books, 2002.

17

Fish Stories

THEME: Books about Fish

PURPOSE: Motivate students to use literature and reference books to learn about fish

MATERIALS:

Selection of fiction and nonfiction books relating to fish, waterways, and fishing

Handouts of scrambled fish names and fish designs

Laminating film

Packages of fish crackers for each class

Colorful fish flies to decorate an old fishing hat

Simple fishing paraphernalia such as a pole (minus the hook), creel, net, wading boots, and a tin can marked WORMS

An easel for posting drawings

STUDENT CONTRIBUTIONS:

Primary grades: a cutout, colored drawing of a fish

Intermediate grades: a short report or story based on research about a specific fish and a cutout, colored drawing of that fish

One intermediate grade: four drawings to accompany a dramatization of *The Fisherman and His Wife* and four students to act out the story

Preparation for Book Event

THREE WEEKS BEFORE THE BOOK EVENT, send out the invitation to staff and students.

When folks go fishing, there are many stories about "the one that got away." Everyone is invited to a FISH STORIES Book Event at the library to celebrate fish and the fun of fishing. Please have several students in your class draw, color, and cut out a fish for our bulletin board. Drawings may range from nine inches to eighteen inches in length. One or two students in each intermediate classroom are requested to research a specific type of fish and write a short one-page report or creative writing story based on research about that fish to share at our Book Event. Reference books are available in a special display in the library. Please bring all reports, stories, and fish drawings to the library within the next two weeks. Come and share fish stories with us!

Invite students from one intermediate class to help dramatize and illustrate *The Fisherman and His Wife* at the Book Event. The following are needed:

- Three actors: the fisherman, his wife, and the flounder
- A stagehand to put up and take down the drawings.
- Four drawings on four separate pieces of large poster board: a small miserable hut, a cottage, a mansion with pillars, and a large stone castle.

Arrange a display of fiction and nonfiction fish books in a special area.

Cut out large bulletin board letters to spell the words FISH STORIES.

Make a sign that reads GONE FISHIN'.

TWO WEEKS BEFORE THE BOOK EVENT, make up a worksheet of scrambled fish names. Locate a worksheet of fish designs suitable for coloring. Run off copies to give to all students at the Book Event.

Borrow fishing paraphernalia such as a fishing hat, fishing flies, a creel, a fishing pole, a net, and waders. Write the word WORMS on an old tin can.

Remind classes that fish pictures and reports are needed by end of the week.

Check with the class helping to dramatize the story to be sure they have drawn pictures and selected three actors and a stagehand.

ONE WEEK BEFORE THE BOOK EVENT, laminate all fish pictures. Punch a hole in them and add invisible thread for hanging. Put blue paper on the bulletin board to represent water, and hang fish from the ceiling in front of it. Add letters to spell FISH STORIES.

Copy student reports and post them along the bottom of the bulletin board.

Decorate an old hat with the fishing flies to wear for the Book Event.

Purchase packages of fish crackers for all classes.

Rehearse *The Fisherman and His Wife* story with students. The librarian or another adult may act as the narrator. Be sure actors have appropriate costumes.

The Fisherman and His Wife

Adapted from original tale by Jakob and Wilhelm Grimm

Characters:

A poor fisherman (wearing fishing hat, carrying fishing pole)
His wife (wearing long dress and apron)
The flounder (wearing fish mask)
Stagehand
Narrator

Narrator: Once there was a poor fisherman and his wife who lived by the sea in a miserable hut. (*Stagehand places picture of hut on easel.)* Every day the fisherman took his fishing pole and went to the sea, hoping to catch a fish for his dinner. *(Fisherman takes pole and pretends to fish.)* One day his line went down, and he caught a very large flounder. When he pulled him in, the fish said,

Flounder: Oh, please, let me go! I am not really a fish. I am an enchanted prince!

Fisherman: Oh, I would never keep a fish that talks! Of course you may go free.

Narrator: So the fisherman let the flounder go, and he went home to his wife with no fish for supper.

Wife: Did you catch any fish today?

Fisherman: The only fish I caught was a flounder that talked. He said he was an enchanted prince so I let him go.

Narrator: The wife was very upset.

Wife: You fool! That was a magic fish! You should have made him give you a wish. Tomorrow you must go back and get a wish from him! I am tired of this miserable hut! Tell him I want a nice little cottage.

Narrator: So the next morning the husband went back to the sea and called the flounder.

Fisherman: Flounder, flounder in the sea,
I have come to beg a boon of thee!
The water bubbled and up came the flounder.

Flounder: What is it that you wish, poor fisherman?

Fisherman: My wife is tired of living in our poor hut. She wishes a nice little cottage.

Flounder: Go home and you shall find your wife in her cottage.

Narrator: The fisherman went home, and there was his wife in their nice little cottage. *(The stagehand replaces the picture of the hut with the picture of the cottage.)* There was a white picket fence and flowers all around it. The wife was happy for a few days, but then she began to want more.

Wife: Husband, I am tired of this tiny little cottage. I want something bigger! Go back and tell the fish I want a mansion.

Fisherman: But, my dear wife, this cottage is just right for us. We do not need a mansion.

Narrator: No matter how long the husband pleaded, the wife would not listen to him. She insisted she wanted a mansion. So the fisherman sighed and returned to the sea to call the flounder.

Fisherman: Flounder, flounder in the sea,
I have come to beg a boon of thee!

Narrator: Soon the water bubbled and up came the flounder.

Flounder: What is that you wish, poor fisherman?

Fisherman: My wife is tired of living in the little cottage. She wishes a mansion.

Flounder: Very well. Go home and you shall find your wife in her mansion.

Narrator: When the fisherman went home, he found his wife happily smiling at him from the marble steps of a huge white mansion with columns and a circular drive. (*The stagehand replaces the picture of the cottage with the picture of the mansion.)* The wife was contented for a few days, but then she began to wish for something more.

Wife: Husband, I am tired of this mansion. I want something bigger. You must go and tell the fish I want a castle.

Fisherman: But, my dear, this mansion is just right for us. We do not need a castle.

Narrator: Again the wife would not listen, so the husband returned to the sea once again.

Fisherman: Flounder, flounder of the sea,
I have come to beg a boon of thee!

Narrator: As before, the water bubbled and up came the flounder. But this time he did not sound quite so pleasant.

Flounder: What is it that you wish, poor fisherman?

Fisherman: My wife is tired of living in the mansion. She wishes a castle.

Flounder: A castle! Very well. Go home and you shall find your wife in her castle.

Narrator: When the fisherman returned home, he found his wife happily seated upon a golden throne in a great stone castle. *(The stagehand replaces the mansion picture with the picture of the castle.)* She was contented for a few days. Then she called her husband to her.

Wife: Husband, I am tired of this castle. I need something bigger. Go back to the fish and tell him I want to be queen of the sun and the moon.

Fisherman: But, my dear wife, this castle is just right for us. You do not need to be queen of the sun and the moon.

Narrator: No matter how long the fisherman pleaded, his wife would not listen. So he returned once more to the sea.

Fisherman: Flounder, flounder of the sea,
I have come to beg a boon of thee!

Narrator: This time the water boiled and bubbled and steam rose from the sea before the flounder appeared.

Flounder: What is it this time, poor fisherman? What does your wife want now?

Fisherman: She is not happy with the castle. She wants to be queen of the sun and the moon.

Flounder: Go home to your wife and do not return. I have granted enough wishes.

Narrator: The flounder disappeared into the sea, never to be seen again. (Stagehand replaces the picture of the castle with the picture of the hut.) When the fisherman returned home, he found his wife in the doorway of their miserable old hut and that is where they lived the rest of their lives. Perhaps there are lessons we might all learn from this tale.

Book Event Activity

Place fishing paraphernalia around the room and wear the old fishing hat. Put up the GONE FISHIN' sign. Welcome everyone to the Book Event to share Fish Stories. Read a short poem about fish or fishing. Discuss the fishing paraphernalia and the sport of fishing in general. Ask whether anyone in the group has gone fishing and what he or she caught. Discuss the concept that sometimes people tell fish stories about "the one that got away." Discuss the fish drawn for the bulletin board, asking the artists to raise their hands if they contributed. Ask students to name types of fish and whether they might be found in fresh or salt water.

Review the rules for good audience behavior briefly and invite the student performers to help you present *The Fisherman and His Wife*. Discuss what lessons might be drawn from the old tale.

Primary grades: Read a fiction fish story such as *McElligot's Pool* by Dr. Seuss, *Swimmy* by Leo Lionni, or *The Rainbow Fish* by Marcus Pfister.

Intermediate grades: Have students read their fish reports and stories to the group. Invite all students to write additional reports and stories about fish or fishing.

Both groups: Give fish puzzle worksheets and packages of fish crackers to each class as they leave.

SCRAMBLED FISH PUZZLE

Directions: Unscramble the following fish names and write them correctly.

1. TORUT ____________________
2. NAUT ____________________
3. BALLHUDE ____________________
4. CHREP ____________________
5. HANARIP ____________________
6. YELLEWA ____________________
7. DOC ____________________
8. INARDES ____________________
9. KRASH ____________________
10. NOWMIN ____________________
11. LEE ____________________
12. LAMNOS ____________________
13. BUTHAIL ____________________
14. SABS ____________________
15. NOTPAR ____________________
16. CLIPREEK ____________________
17. EPIK ____________________
18. RANILM ____________________
19. LOUDNERF ____________________
20. CHODKAD ____________________

Answers: 1. trout 2. tuna 3. bullhead 4. perch 5. piranha 6. walleye 7. cod 8. sardine 9. shark 10. minnow 11. eel 12. salmon 13. halibut 14. bass 15. tarpon 16. pickerel 17. pike 18. marlin 19. flounder 20. haddock

Suggested Bibliography for Fish Theme

Primary Grades

Arenson, Roberta. *Manu and the Talking Fish.* New York: Barefoot Books, 2000.

Asch, Frank. *Moonbear's Pet.* New York: Simon & Schuster Books for Young Readers, 1997.

Franklin, Kristine L. *The Gift.* San Francisco: Chronicle Books, 1999.

Joosse, Barbara M. *I Love You the Purplest.* San Francisco: Chronicle Books, 1996.

Kimmel, Eric A. *Anansi Goes Fishing.* New York: Holiday House, 1992.

Krudop, Walter. *The Man Who Caught Fish.* New York: Farrar, Straus and Giroux, 2000.

Lee, Justin. *How To Draw Fish.* New York: PowerKids Press, 2002.

Nicolai, Margaret. *Kitaq Goes Ice Fishing.* Anchorage: Alaska Northwest Books, 1998.

Nolen, Jerdine. *Max and Jax in Second Grade.* San Diego: Silver Whistle/Harcourt, 2002.

Page, Deborah. *Orcas Around Me: My Alaskan Summer.* Morton Grove, IL: Albert Whitman, 1997.

Pfeffer, Wendy. *What's It Like To Be a Fish?* New York: Harper-Collins, 1996.

Pfister, Marcus. *The Rainbow Fish.* New York: North-South Books, 1992.

Polacco, Patricia. *Luba and the Wren.* New York: Philomel Books, 1999.

San Souci, Robert D. *Six Foolish Fishermen.* New York: Hyperion Books for Children, 2000.

Seuss, Dr. *McElligot's Pool.* New York: Random House, 1974.

———. *One Fish, Two Fish, Red Fish, Blue Fish.* New York: Random House, 1988.

Sloat, Teri. *There Was an Old Lady Who Swallowed a Trout!* New York: Henry Holt, 1998.

Van Laan, Nancy. *Little Fish, Lost.* New York: Atheneum Books for Young Readers, 1998.

Wells, Rosemary. *The Fisherman and His Wife: A Brand New Version.* New York: Dial Books for Young Readers, 1998.

Intermediate Grades

Bailey, Jill. *How Fish Swim.* New York: Benchmark Books, 1997.

Borden, Louise. *The Little Ships: The Heroic Rescue at Dunkirk in World War II.* New York: Margaret K. McElderry Books, 1997.

Gilbert, Carter Rowell. *National Audubon Society Field Guide to Fishes. North America.* New York: Knopf, 2002.

Hirschi, Ron. *Salmon.* Minneapolis, MN: Carolrhoda Books, 2000.

Hyde, Dayton O. *The Major, the Poacher, and the Wonderful One-trout River.* New York: Boyds Mills Press, 1998.

Jackson, Lawrence. *Newfoundland & Labrador.* Minneapolis, MN: Lerner Publications, 1995.

Johnson, Jinny. *Simon & Schuster Children's Guide to Sea Creatures.* New York: Simon & Schuster Books for Young Readers, 1998.

Kalman, Bobbie. *What Is a Fish?* New York: Crabtree, 1998.

Landau, Elaine. *Piranhas.* New York: Children's Press, 1999.

———. *Siamese Fighting Fish.* New York: Children's Press, 1999.

London, Jonathan. *Where the Big Fish Are.* Cambridge, MA: Candlewick, 2001.

Makowski, Robin Lee. *How To Draw Sea Creatures.* Vero Beach, FL: Rourke, 2002.

McMillan, Bruce. *Salmon Summer.* Boston: Houghton Mifflin, 1998.

Ricciuti, Edward R. *What On Earth Is a Pout?* Woodbridge, CT: Blackbirch Press, 1997.

Ross, Kathy. *Crafts for Kids Who Are Wild about Oceans.* Brookfield, CT: Millbrook Press, 1998.

Savage, Stephen. *Fish.* Austin, TX: Raintree Steck-Vaughn, 2000.

Smith, C. Lovett. *National Audubon Society Field Guide to Tropical Marine Fishes of the Caribbean, the Gulf of Mexico, Florida, the Bahamas, and Bermuda.* New York: Knopf, 1997.

Snedden, Robert. *What Is a Fish?* San Francisco: Sierra Club Books for Children, 1997.

Souza, D.M. *Fish That Play Tricks.* Minneapolis, MN: Carolrhoda Books, 1998.

Walker, Sally M. *Fossil Fish Found Alive.* Minneapolis, MN: Carolrhoda Books, 2002.

Williams, Sarah. *101 Facts about Tropical Fish.* Milwaukee, WI: Gareth Stevens, 2001.

18

I Spy the Mystery Reader

This chapter varies slightly from previous chapters in that it is designed to be a generic event that can be modified as an introduction to schoolwide reading promotions such as read-a-thons, summer reading programs, Read Across America Day or Children's Book Week.

THEME: Students Search for the Mystery Reader Around the School and Learn about the Reading Promotion

PURPOSE: Motivate students to participate in the schoolwide reading promotion

MATERIALS:

A colorful vest

Large shoeboxes (one for each grade level)

Paper ballots for student entries

New paperback books of various reading and interest levels (at least two for every grade level)

Reading record sheets, certificates, and bookmarks for students

STUDENT CONTRIBUTION:

Written ballots recording sightings of the Mystery Reader and participation in the reading promotion

Preparation for Book Event

THREE WEEKS BEFORE THE BOOK EVENT, order or make reading record sheets, certificates, and bookmarks for the students participating in the reading promotion. Motivational materials are available from companies such as Upstart at www.highsmith.com, DEMCO at www.demco.com, or can be created by hand. Run off permission slips for participation if they are required.

TWO WEEKS BEFORE THE BOOK EVENT, send out the invitation to staff and students.

> You are invited to a kickoff Book Event in the library to begin our annual reading promotion. Watch for the Mystery Reader around the school any time next week. The Reader will be wearing a special vest and reading a book. If you spy any of the Mystery Readers, do not disturb them. Just fill out one of the ballots enclosed with this invitation, bring it to the library, and place it in the box for your grade level. Someone from your grade will win a wonderful new book at the Book Event. Sharpen your spy skills and keep your eyes open for the Mystery Reader. And be sure and sign up for the reading promotion after the Book Event!

Decorate a colorful vest with feathers, sequins, reading buttons, etc. Wear the vest or display it in the library to stimulate interest.

Decorate a ballot box for each grade level with bright paper. Label it with the words MYSTERY READER and a grade level.

Duplicate many copies of the following ballot. Enclose some with the invitations and keep a surplus in the library.

I SPY THE MYSTERY READER

WHO? ____
(Name or Description)

WHERE? ______________________________________

MY NAME______________________________________

MY GRADE_____________________________________

Collect at least two new paperback books for each grade level to allow students a choice for prizes.

Solicit about fifteen volunteer staff members and students to act as the Mystery Reader. The Reader will wear the vest, sit in a specified area of the school at a prearranged time, and read quietly for five to ten minutes. Compile a list of volunteers, their respective reading spots, and their reading times in chronological order.

Cut out large bulletin board letters to spell I SPY MYSTERY READER and smaller letters to spell JOIN THE READING PROMOTION.

Collect pictures or posters of children and adults reading.

Gather colorful book jackets.

A WEEK BEFORE THE BOOK EVENT, remind staff and students to be on the alert for the Mystery Reader around the school.

Give each Mystery Reader a copy of the list of readers. They should don the vest, read for five to ten minutes at their specified time and place, and then pass the vest on to the next reader on the list.

Decorate the bulletin board with cutout letters, book jackets, and pictures of people reading. Add a sample of the student reading record, certificate, and bookmark for the reading promotion.

Create a display of library books about the importance of reading. See the bibliography for suggestions.

Select a picture book from this display to read to the students at the Book Event. Possible choices could be books by Patricia Polacco such as *Thank You, Mr. Falker, Aunt Chip and the Great Triple Creek Dam Affair,* and *The Bee Tree. Library Lil* by Suzanne Williams and *The Wednesday Surprise* by Eve Bunting are other possibilities.

Choose a short poem about reading or books to welcome the students to the Book Event. Suggestions might include "The Land of Story Books" by Robert Louis Stevenson, "The Library" by Barbara A. Huff, "Jimmy Jet and His TV Set" by Shel Silverstein, or "Pages" by Douglas Florian.

Book Event Activity

Display the free paperback books on a nearby table and the ballot boxes in front of the group. Welcome everyone to the Book Event, wearing the Mystery Reader vest. Read the short poem about reading or books.

Discuss the fun of spying the Mystery Reader around the school and ask students to tell about their sightings.

Choose someone to draw one winner of a free paperback book from each of the ballot boxes whose grade levels are in attendance at that time. Winners may make their selections after the Book Event is over. Post the names of the winners for everyone to see.

Read a picture book about the importance of reading to the group. Discuss the relevance of the book and reading to everyday life. Show some titles from the book display, suggesting that students may want to begin the reading promotion with one of them.

Explain the procedure for the reading promotion and encourage all students to participate. Point out the reading record they will complete and the certificate they will win. Explain the permission slip if it is required. All of these materials may be given to classroom teachers to be distributed to the students later. Wish the students well and assure them that you will follow their progress with great interest. Send them on their way with the gift bookmarks.

Suggested Bibliography for Mystery Reader Theme

Primary Grades

Bertram, Debbie. *The Best Place to Read.* New York: Random House, 2003.

Bloom, Becky. *Wolf!* New York: Orchard Books, 1999.

Bruss, Deborah. *Book! Book! Book!* New York: A.A. Levine, 2001.

Bunting, Eve. *The Wednesday Surprise.* New York: Clarion Books, 1989.

Charlip, Remy. *Why I Will Never Ever Ever Ever Have Enough Time To Read This Book.* Berkeley, CA: Tricycle, 2000.

Conover, Chris. *The Lion's Share.* New York: Farrar, Straus and Giroux, 2000.

Deedy, Carmen Agra. *The Library Dragon.* Atlanta: Peachtree, 1994.

Ernst, Lisa Campbell. *Stella Louella's Runaway Book.* New York: Simon & Schuster Books for Young Readers, 1998.

Fox, Mem. *A Bedtime Story.* Greenvale, NY: Mondo, 1996.

Hoban, Lillian. *Arthur's Prize Reader.* New York: Harper & Row, 1978.

McPhail, David M. *Edward and the Pirates.* Boston: Little, Brown, 1997.

Meddaugh, Susan. *Hog-Eye.* Boston: Houghton Mifflin, 1995.

Meister, Cari. *Tiny Goes to the Library.* New York: Viking, 2000.

Polacco, Patricia. *Aunt Chip and the Great Triple Creek Dam Affair.* New York: Philomel Books, 1996.

———. *The Bee Tree.* New York: Putnam & Grosset, 1998.

Stevens, Janet. *And the Dish Ran Away with the Spoon.* San Diego: Harcourt, 2001.

Stewart, Sarah. *The Library.* New York: Farrar, Straus and Giroux, 1995.

Wick, Walter. *I Spy School Days: A Book of Picture Riddles.* New York: Scholastic Books, 1995.

Williams, Suzanne. *Library Lil.* New York: Dial Books for Young Readers, 1997.

Intermediate Grades

Avi. *Prairie School.* New York: HarperCollins, 2001.

Borden, Louise. *The Day Eddie Met the Author.* New York: Margaret K. McElderry Books, 2001.

Bradby, Marie. *More Than Anything Else.* New York: Orchard Books, 1995.

Cleary, Beverly. *Dear Mr. Henshaw.* New York: Avon Books, 1994.

———. *Muggie Maggie.* New York: Avon, 1991.

Handford, Martin. *Where's Waldo?* Cambridge, MA: Candlewick Press, 1997.

Kinsey-Warnock, Natalie. *Lumber Camp Library.* New York: HarperCollins, 2002.

Lowry, Lois. *Zooman Sam.* Boston: Houghton Mifflin, 1999.

Manes, Stephen. *Be a Perfect Person in Just Three Days!* New York: Clarion Books, 1982.

Miller, William. *Richard Wright and the Library Card.* New York. Lee & Low Books, 1997.

Polacco, Patricia. *Thank You, Mr. Falker.* New York: Philomel Books, 1998.

San Souci, Robert D. *A Weave of Words: An Armenian Tale.* New York: Orchard Books, 1998.

Scieszka, Jon. *Summer Reading Is Killing Me!* New York: Viking, 1998.

Steiner, Joan. *Look-Alikes.* Boston: Little, Brown, 1998.

Tripp, Valcrie. *Josefina Learns a Lesson: A School Story.* Middleton, WI: Pleasant Company, 1997.

Wilson, Nancy Hope. *Old People, Frogs, and Albert.* New York: Farrar, Straus and Giroux, 1997.

Additional Readings

Bauer, Caroline Feller. *Read for the Fun of It: Active Programming with Books for Children.* Bronx, NY: H. W. Wilson, 1992.

The Complete Grimm's Fairy Tales. New York: Pantheon Books, 1972.

Frost, Robert. *The Road Not Taken: A Selection of Robert Frost's Poems.* New York: Holt, Rinehart, and Winston, 1985.

Gillespie, John Thomas. *Best Books for Children: Preschool Through Grade 6.* Westport, CT: Bowker-Greenwood, 2002.

Inventions and Inventors (ten volumes). Danbury, CT: Grolier Educational, 2000.

Lima, Carolyn W. *A to Zoo: Subject Access to Children's Picture Books.* Westport, CT: Bowker-Greenwood, 2001.

MacDonald, Margaret Read. *Bookplay: 101 Creative Themes To Share with Young Children.* North Haven, CT: Library Professional Publications, 1995.

Matthews, Tom L. *Always Inventing: A Photobiography of Alexander Graham Bell.* Washington, DC: National Geographic Society, 1999.

Osborne, Mary Pope. *American Tall Tales.* New York: Alfred A. Knopf, 1991.

Yans-McLaughlin and Marjorie Lightman. *Ellis Island and the Peopling of America.* New York: New Press, 1997.

Index